A Quaker's Tour
of the Colonial Northeast and Canada

The 1773 Travel Journals
of Jabez Maud Fisher of Philadelphia

Jabez Maud Fisher

A Quaker's Tour of the Colonial Northeast and Canada

The 1773 Travel Journals
of Jabez Maud Fisher of Philadelphia

Jack Campisi
and
William A. Starna

Editors

American Philosophical Society Press
Philadelphia • 2014

Transactions of the
American Philosophical Society
Held at Philadelphia
For Promoting Useful Knowledge
Volume 104, Part 4

ISBN: 978-1-60618-044-0
US ISSN: 0065-9746

Library of Congress Cataloguing-in-Publication Data

Fisher, Jabez Maud, 1750-1779.
   A Quaker's tour of the colonial northeast and Canada : the 1773 travel
journals of Jabez Maud Fisher of Philadelphia / edited by Jack Campisi and
William A. Starna.
      pages cm. — (Transactions of the American Philosophical Society
held at Philadelphia for promoting useful knowledge, ISSN 0065-9746 ;
volume 104, part 4)
   Includes bibliographical references and index.
   ISBN 978-1-60618-044-0
   1. Fisher, Jabez Maud, 1750-1779—Diaries. 2. Fisher, Jabez Maud, 1750-
1779—Travel—Northeastern States. 3. Fisher, Jabez Maud, 1750-1779—
Travel—Canada. 4. Northeastern States—Description and travel—Early
works to 1800. 5. Canada—Description and travel—Early works to 1800. I.
Campisi, Jack, editor. II. Starna, William A., editor. III. Title. IV. Title: 1773
travel journals of Jabez Maud Fisher of Philadelphia.
   E163.F53 2014
   917.1904—dc23
                        2014039550

Contents

Acknowledgments

A work of this scope could not have been completed without the contributions and good will of the many institutions, scholars, colleagues, and friends from whom we sought assistance. First and foremost, we would like to extend our thanks to the staff of the Friends Historical Library of Swarthmore College, and in particular its curator, Christopher Densmore, who granted us permission to publish the Fisher journals and who provided valuable insights into the history of the Fisher family of Philadelphia. Institutions in New York State that aided in our research include the Oneida Historical Society, the Herkimer County Historical Society, the Rome Historical Society, the Montgomery County Department of History and Archives, and the Oswego County Historical Society. We thank the staff of these institutions, most of whom are volunteers, for their help in chasing down information that was often obscure and difficult to find, only a portion of which we eventually used, but all of which we found fascinating and valuable as background.

We are also grateful to the following persons who were more than generous in offering us their expertise: Jere Brubaker, Old Fort Niagara; David Cohen, independent scholar; Kate Deviny, Westfield Athenaeum, Westfield, Massachusetts; Charles Gehring, New Netherland Research Center, Albany, New York; George Hamell, Rock Foundation, Rochester, New York; Scott Meachum, independent scholar; Ray Middleton, Leeds Quakers, Leeds, United Kingdom; and Oliver Pickering, Yorkshire Quaker Archives, Leeds University Library, Leeds, United Kingdom.

We would also like to acknowledge Sandra Cadwalader of Philadelphia; Arthur and Mary Hornett of New Hartford, New York; and Robert and Lorraine Loomis of Frankfort, New York. They endured our repeated tales about Fisher's journey—the people he met on the way, descriptions of his diet "on the road," and his passion for waterfalls. We thank them for their patience and interest.

We reserve special thanks to Paris residents Cynthia Schoch, a long-time family friend; and her seafaring husband, Alain Bernard, who researched and translated for us the song "La Femme du President."

We also are grateful to Eileen M. McClafferty, who read and offered helpful comments on early drafts of our manuscript; and Julia Campisi, who prepared the index. The map was skillfully drawn and produced for us by Kate Simeon. We also would like to thank two of the readers solicited by the American Philosophical Society, Susan E. Klepp and Karim Tiro, for their constructive suggestions to improve our work.

Finally, we dedicate this work to Beverly Anne Campisi, who gave the editors her untiring support, but who did not live to see its publication.

Illustrations

Introduction

The year was 1773, and the British colonies of North America were alive with the disquieting voices of rebellion. That May Parliament passed the Tea Act, which generated opposition in the colonies and by year's end provoked a famous and not-so-civil disobedience in Boston harbor. Over the previous decade, a flurry of unpopular laws and policies promulgated by Parliament had set many citizens on edge, in particular those who increasingly resented the at-a-distance authority of the Crown. However, it was the Stamp Act of 1765 that prompted the formation in each colony of Committees of Correspondence. As fledgling shadow governments, they would spearhead a collective resistance to British actions, leading in early autumn 1774 to the creation of the First Continental Congress. Two years later the thirteen colonies would announce their declaration of independence from the Crown.

The year 1773 was also when Jabez Maud Fisher, a twenty-three-year-old Quaker and an unnamed companion (or companions) set out from Philadelphia for New York City and then to Albany. It was the beginning of a journey that would take Fisher as far west as Fort Erie, across the Niagara River from the frontier outpost that would take the name Buffalo; north to Montreal, Trois-Rivières, and Quebec, now all within the Province of Quebec, created by the Royal Proclamation of 1763; and finally, to Boston and Newport, Rhode Island. Over the course of his five months of travel, Fisher and his party walked, rode, or boated something short of 2,000 miles, following alongside or on the Hudson, Mohawk, and St. Lawrence Rivers, as well as on Lakes Ontario, Champlain, and George. Fisher would pass through or linger on the way in hamlets, towns, cities, forts, trading houses, and native communities. He would meet and, with uneven interest, interact with a mix of people, a sample of colonial citizenry—merchants, judges, tavern keepers, politicians, clergy, *coureurs de bois*, intellectuals, wealthy landowners, soldiers, farmers, boatmen, and government officials, in addition to the country's original inhabitants, American Indians. In keeping with what was apparently a family tradition—Fisher's brothers all kept journals of their travels—Fisher recorded his observations and escapades in a day journal, leaving for us a chronicle of life at a very auspicious time in American history.[1] It begins on

---

[1]Kenneth Morgan, ed., *An American Quaker in the British Isles: The Travel Journals of Jabez Maud Fisher, 1775–1779* (New York: Oxford University Press, 1992), 3–4.

the road, as it were, on June 18, 1773, and ends abruptly in Newport on October 3 of the same year, some time before Fisher returned to Philadelphia.

Jabez Maud Fisher was born of Quaker parents in Philadelphia on September 10, 1750, the second youngest of his three brothers and three sisters.[2] His father, Joshua Fisher (1707–83), who began his working life as a modestly prosperous hatmaker, and mother, Sarah Rowland (1716–72), had married and lived for thirteen years in Lewes, near Cape Henlopen, Delaware. In 1746 the family moved to Philadelphia, where, within a few short years, Joshua established a mercantile business—Joshua Fisher & Sons—on that city's waterfront. He also founded a shipping line whose packet ships were the first to regularly sail from the port of Philadelphia to London. Of related interest is that in about 1756, with the help of his brother-in-law Samuel Rowland, Joshua applied his skills as a nautical surveyor, producing the first authoritative chart of Delaware Bay and the Delaware River.[3]

There is nothing known of Jabez Maud Fisher's life before his 1773 journey. More curious is that there is also nothing known of the reasons behind his sojourn, whether from family sources or as expressed in Jabez's journal itself. It might be surmised that his father and older brothers sent him off to assess how businesses were faring in the colonies or to learn of economic opportunities that might be had at a distance from Philadelphia, especially given the changes that were sure to follow should the rumblings of a revolt against the Crown become a reality. Still, although the visits he made to important centers of commerce, such as Montreal, Quebec, Boston, and Newport, would have made sense, it is somewhat difficult to explain the leg of the trip that took him far to the west and the Niagara region. Or was the journey that he undertook simply of a sporting nature, something that a young, well-educated man from a family of means might do, a sort of "see-the-world" excursion?

To a noticeable degree, Fisher's day journal is one of easy observation, painting a picture of a light-hearted yet matter-of-fact adventure. There is little hint of the self-reflection or musings of a diarist. Fisher seems captivated by most of what he sees, exhibiting a particular fascination with waterfalls, which he measures, climbs around, and describes in rapturous detail, moving him to wax poetic in his writing and enter among the pages of his journal a recitation of a well-known verse on nature. There were military posts, new

---

[2] Jabez's sister Sarah, the youngest of the seven siblings, was born in 1759. See Morgan, *An American Quaker*, fig. facing 1.

[3] Anna Wharton Smith, *Genealogy of the Fisher Family, 1682 to 1896* (Philadelphia, 1896), 22–27.

and old, to explore, manned by undoubtedly colorful career soldiers and their officers; ubiquitous inns in which to lodge and partake of the victuals and perhaps the drink they offered; and architecturally elaborate estates and gardens of the gentry to wander around and marvel about.

Fisher's journals do not reach the scope and detail of explorer and naturalist Peter Kalm's famous travels through Pennsylvania, New York, and Canada, published in English in 1770; or fur trader Alexander Henry's adventures in Canada between the years 1760 and 1776; or Richard Smith's 1769 tour of New York Colony's four great rivers. Nor is it as rough and ready as Warren Johnson's 1760–61 chronicle of his visit to his brother, Sir William Johnson, and New York's Mohawk Valley, or as urbane as Count Paolo Adreani's 1790 journey through New York Colony and Iroquoia. And there is nothing of the political intrigue such as that found in the journals of fellow Quakers William Savery and James Emlen while attending the Treaty of Canandaigua two decades later. Nonetheless, Fisher's journals do present a different man's experiences and perspectives, in this case those of a young Quaker from a well-to-do and respected Philadelphia family, on frontier and city life in parts of northeastern North America.[4]

Adding to the exotic bent of Fisher's experiences were the American Indians whom he encountered here and there on the trail and on the St. Lawrence River while he tarried in their villages. Native people in the region— Iroquoians and Algonquians, the latter groups living primarily in New England and the Hudson Valley—had suffered greatly from the ravages of the French and Indian War (Seven Years' War), which had ended a decade earlier. Nonetheless, numbers of Indian people remained in their homelands,

---

[4]See Adolph B. Benson, rev. ed., Peter Kalm's *Travels in North America: The English Version of 1770* (New York: Dover, 1987); Warren Johnson, "Journal of Warren Johnson." In *In Mohawk Country: Narratives of a Native People*, eds. Dean R. Snow, Charles T. Gehring, and William A. Starna (Syracuse: Syracuse University Press, 1996), 250–73; James Bain, ed., *Travels and Adventures in Canada and the Indian Territories Between the Years 1760 and 1776, by Alexander Henry, Fur Trader* (Boston: Little, Brown, 1901); Francis W. Halsey, ed., *A Tour of the Hudson, the Mohawk, the Susquehanna, and the Delaware in 1769, Being the Journal of Richard Smith of Burlington, New Jersey* (1906; repr. Fleischmanns NY: Purple Mountain Press, 1989); Cesare Marino and Karim M. Tiro, eds. and trans., *Along the Hudson and Mohawk: The 1790 Journey of Count Paolo Andreani* (Philadelphia: University of Pennsylvania Press, 2006); Paolo Adreani, "Travels of a Gentleman from Milan." In *In Mohawk Country: Narratives of a Native People*, eds. Dean R. Snow, Charles T. Gehring, and William A. Starna (Syracuse: Syracuse University Press, 1996), 318–33; William Savery, *A Journal of the Life, Travels, and Religious Labours of William Savery* (Comp. Jonathan Evans. C. Gilpin: London, 1844); William N. Fenton, "The Journal of James Emlen Kept on a Trip to Canandaigua, New York," *Ethnohistory* 12, no. 4 (1965): 279–342. For a bibliography of the numerous and varied diaries and travel journals written before 1861, consult William Mathews, comp., *American Diaries: An Annotated Bibliography of American Diaries Written Before 1861* (Berkeley: University of California Press, 1945).

whereas others found themselves in refugee communities scattered principally throughout the Susquehanna River Valley of New York and far-northern Pennsylvania. On the other hand, the Roman Catholic missions that Fisher visited on the St. Lawrence, the first at St. Regis (Akwesasne), established about 1750, and the second, downriver at Caughnawaga (Kahnawake), begun nearly a century earlier, had been havens for native people for decades. Indians, too, would be caught up in the Revolution, which would bring widespread devastation to their people and communities, and for those many Iroquois who would support the Crown, compel their flight into Canada.[5]

What is surprising, however, is the absence of any mention by Fisher of the political goings-on of the day. This is in spite of his meeting and socializing with the many personalities who already were or were fast becoming key figures in both the Patriot and Loyalist causes. This was especially the case during his time in Boston and Newport, where he hobnobbed with men occupying the full range of political and activist leanings—men who would be among the signers of the Constitution; others whose fealty to the Crown caused them to be banished from the colonies; a justice who heard the case of the Boston Massacre; a soon-to-be general in the Revolution who would become governor of New Hampshire; a future member of the Massachusetts Senate Convention for the adoption of the 1788 Constitution; and the Royal Navy admiral who would enforce Crown law promulgated in response to the Boston Tea Party, along with the very owner of one of the ships from whose decks those now-celebrated chests of tea would be tossed into the bay. Yet, how is it that Fisher could sit down with such a collection of notable persons, listen to what had to have been the politically charged conversations swirling about him, and write not one word about any of it?

Before the Revolution, the company of Joshua Fisher & Sons had grown to be the most successful and profitable Quaker merchant house in Philadelphia, due in considerable part to the expansion of its manufacturing and merchandising interests not only in the colonies, but also in Great Britain.[6] Indeed, in the mid-1760s, Jabez's brothers had traveled to Britain to assess its manufacturing and trading environment and also forge what might prove to be helpful social ties to the community of Friends. Jabez, as we will shortly see, would also find his way there, but for different reasons.

---

[5]See Colin G. Calloway, *The American Revolution in Indian Country: Crisis and Diversity in Native American Communities* (Cambridge: Cambridge University Press, 1995); Barbara Graymont, *The Iroquois in the American Revolution* (Syracuse: Syracuse University Press, 1972).

[6]The discussion that follows is drawn from Morgan, *American Quaker*, 1–26.

Led by their pacifist principles, many Quakers in Philadelphia would stand in opposition to the War of Independence. Although a number of the city's several hundred Quakers reportedly took up arms in support of the Patriots, the majority held to their neutrality, while nevertheless hoping for a British victory. The Fishers were no exception. In addition to refusing military service, many Quakers resisted funding the war by withholding taxes and boycotting the continental currency, Jabez's brother Samuel being one of the notable dissenters.

By 1774, Jabez Maud Fisher was regarded as one of Philadelphia's most active conservatives. As Kenneth Morgan has it, in spring 1775 he was "publicly rebuked for submitting an anonymous letter to the *Pennsylvania Ledger* that questioned the commitment of a county in neighboring Delaware to Congressional policy," a piece that found its way to newspapers in New York and elsewhere in Pennsylvania.[7] Jabez's father decided to act. Believing, probably rightly so, that his outspoken son would be safer out of the country, he sent him on the next available ship to London. There he was to establish commercial connections for the company with merchants whose goods could be marketed in Philadelphia. He would spend more than three years traveling through the British Isles and parts of Northern Europe.[8] It is difficult, then, not to draw the conclusion that it was Jabez's evolving Loyalist leanings that caused him to (wisely?) leave out of his journal of 1773 whatever he saw or heard of the portent and people of revolution, especially during his sojourn in Boston and Newport.

Jabez attempted to return home in May 1778 after he learned that the family's business had been closed by Philadelphia's Council of Safety for its refusal to accept continental bills of credit as payment. Moreover, his brothers and several other relatives had either been exiled to Virginia or jailed for what were considered to be their subversive activities. And there was the not unimportant matter of being away from his fiancée, Hannah Redwood. However, for Fisher, the clearly unfavorable political climate in the colonies was enough to prevent him from getting any nearer to home than New York

---

[7] Ibid., 4. See also Fisher's revealing letter to Joseph Galloway (1731–1803), a delegate from Pennsylvania to the First Continental Congress, who shifted his allegiance during the Revolution and lived the remainder of his life in Britain; [Jabez Maud Fisher], "More Galloway Letters," *Historical Magazine* July 1862: 204–5. We thank Susan Klepp for directing us to this reference.

[8] The journals kept by Jabez Maud Fisher during his travels in Great Britain are published. See Morgan, *American Quaker*.

City, forcing him to sail back to London six months later. He would die of scarlet fever at Leeds House on December 1, 1779.[9]

Fisher's journals are in the collection of the Friends Historical Library, Swarthmore College, Swarthmore, Pennsylvania, accessioned as follows: Journal of a Trip to Canada 4 Vols., Joseph Wharton Papers, Record Group 5/162, Box 9, Ser. 1-B Jabez M. Fisher (1750). Volumes one, two, and four are 18 x 12 cm and covered in leather, whereas volume three, covered in marbled paper, is 20 x 14 cm. All four of the loose-leaf volumes appear to have been compiled at or near the time of the events described. In the 1970s the journals became part of the Wharton and Fisher family papers through the courtesy of Catharine (Wharton) Morris Wright (1899–1988). A noted watercolorist, Catharine was a granddaughter of Joseph Wharton (1826–1909), founder of the Wharton School at the University of Pennsylvania, cofounder of Bethlehem Steel, and a founder of Swarthmore College.[10]

In February 1909, a typescript of the Fisher journals was given to the Oneida Historical Society, Utica, New York, by C. [Chauncey] Loomis Allen (1870–1941), then vice president and general manager of the Syracuse Rapid Transit Railway Company.[11] Allen wrote that he had been granted access to the journals by William Redwood Wright (1846–1914) of Philadelphia, whose son, Sidney Longstreth Wright, Jr. (1896–1970), would marry Catharine (Wharton) Morris, just mentioned. The journals apparently came into Catharine's hands after her father's death, soon after which they were gifted to the Friends Historical Library.

The transcript of the Fisher journals presented here was produced from the original and photocopies of the original. In those places in the original where we found Fisher's handwriting difficult to read or obscured, we referred to C. Loomis Allen's 1909 typescript for clues. Fisher's spelling, capitalization, punctuation, syntax, and grammar, in addition to his abbreviations, notations, and slips of the pen, have been faithfully reproduced and are, in most cases, absent emendation. Strike-outs by Fisher have been retained, his interlinear insertions marked by "^." References to words or letters that Fisher crossed

---

[9]The Yorkshire Quarterly Meeting register contains the following entry on Fisher's death: "Fisher, Jabez Maud. [Date of death:] 1779 12 1. [Age:] Supposed 28. [Residence:] Philadelphia in province of Pennsylvania, died in Leeds. [Description:] Merchant. [Monthly meeting:] Brighouse [the monthly meeting to which Leeds belonged]. [Date of burial:] 1779 12 3. [Place of burial:] Meadow Lane, Leeds." The burial ground at Meadow Lane was closed in 1868. Today the site is occupied by the headquarters of the supermarket chain Asda, owned by Walmart. Oliver Pickering, personal communication, Sept. 2, 2011. Hannah Redwood (1759–96) would marry Charles Wharton (1743–1838) in Philadelphia in 1784.

[10]Christopher Densmore, letter to Jack Campisi, August 29, 2011.

[11]C. Loomis Allen to Oneida Historical Society, February 17, 1909.

out are in brackets, as are editorial comments on the legibility and condition of the manuscript. Also in brackets is the occasional clarification of spellings, contractions, and abbreviations. Throughout, every effort was made to identify persons and places, and are so footnoted. As readers will discover, those efforts were not always successful. We would add that no attempt was made to guess the identities of persons whom Fisher lists only by their initials.

Finally, between each manuscript page of the journal is a sheet of blotting paper of the same dimensions and color as the pages. Fisher wrote random comments of various lengths on the blotters, perhaps as addenda or afterthoughts to what he had entered on the manuscript pages. We have placed these comments in brackets, italicized and underlined, in the text of the journal where we believe they best fit.

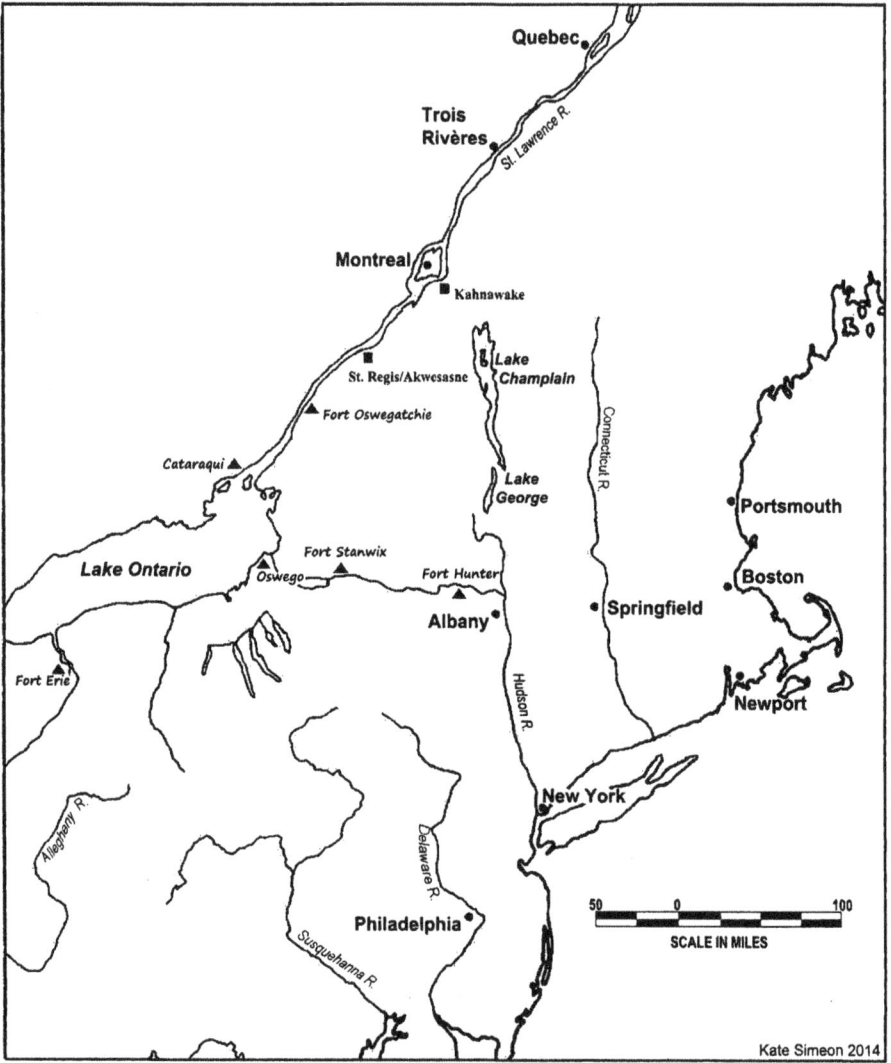

Map of area traveled by Jabez Maud Fisher.

Fisher's Journals

VOLUME ONE

Distances to Places cont. in this Book

6th Day June 18th 1773 —

Set off from Philadelphia in Co. with R: D: in the N[ew] York Stage for
that Place — we breakfasted at the Sign of Wheat Sheaf abt. 8 Miles from
Phila. — from thence set off reach'd Bristol abt. 10 & went to Burlington,
came back to Bristol ~~by~~ where we shifted the Horses & set off for Trenton
on arrival at the Ferry we found a Chair[1] sent by J:W: with an Invitation
to dine with him which we accepted. from thence we went to ~~Trent~~
Princeton where we went to see the College which stands on a pretty
Eminence & commands an extensive Prospect. The Building is abt. 200
feet front by 50 Deep, 4 Stories high. There are on each Floor 14 Rooms
in which there are 2 Schollars — besides a convenient Hall for public
Orations &c. The Situation is Healthy & the Country round about it
tolerably good, ~~but the~~ [ten lines crossed out] [two pages missing] he had
heard of our Intention to come, but not finding him at home altho he left
Word for us to stay there in case we should call while he was out. we
determin'd tho late at Night to take another March in quest of a Bed,
which we soon after found tho' a very indifferent dirty House however
the Fatigue of the Journey, soon suffer'd Morpheus[2] to close our wearied
Eyelids —

June 20th.

Rose early this Morning took a Walk up the East River[3] abt. 1/2 Mile
passing thro all the Ship Yards in our Way, where ~~th~~ were
only 2 Ships building we ^saw^ likewise the Keel of a large Dutch India
Man[4] laid 138 feet ~~that~~ from hence we went to bathe. came to our
Lodging breakfasted when we were waited on by RB: with a D. Invitation
from our very hospitable fr'd W F — which we accepted — went to
meeting in the Morning din'd at home (W F's) & again in the Afternoon,
after Meeting drank tea with J W: sup'd at home —

---

[1]Chair: a light vehicle drawn by a single horse, a chaise.
[2]In Greek mythology, the god of dreams.
[3]The East River, separating Long Island from Manhattan Island and the Bronx.
[4]Apparently a ship of the Dutch East Indian Company.

21st.

This Morning having fixed upon a Party [*J C. with W & J F. & J Foxcroft*] to go to Black ^Point^[5] by Water. we got ready, & abt. 4 in the After sat off in J F's boat which he built on purpose for pleasuring & by Sun Set reach'd black Point which is abt. 45 Mile distant, & most of the Way again a strong tide of Flood — here we lay at Anchor all Night — a high swell in the Sea —

22d.

Rose abt. Sun Rise & began to fish, 7 of us in Co [*in Co. with ourselves & R B Lily & J Watson, B: Thom & J Burling*] they caught them very fast for the most part Sea Bass some Black Fish &c by 12 O Clock after hav'g all eat a hearty Breakfast & Dinner we weighd Anchor with 800 Fish, & got up to N York abt. 7 in the Evening; spent this Evening with J W: —

23 —

This Morning we fixd a Party of 4 & agreed to take an equal Number of Girls, accordingly we sallied out invited the Girls who accepted the Invitation & hav.g din'd with H:H: we got up from the table to look out for horses & Chairs wch we easily found & abt. 4 O Clock cross'd the Ferry at Paulus Hook[6] where we drank tea, intending that Night to go as far as New Ark [Newark] on our Way to Pasaick [Passaic] Falls,[7] but on our Arrival there it being Court time we could not procure a Lodging & were oblig'd to get a Tavern abt. 3 Mile further on, which we reach'd 1/2 past 9 — & got pretty well entertain'd —

24th.

Rose early this Morning & set of[f] for the Accomplishment of the Rout. & reachd Pasaick abt. 7 0 Cl which is 27 Miles from N York

---

[5]Black Point, at the confluence of the Shrewsbury and Navesink Rivers in Shrewsbury Township, Monmouth County, NJ; Thomas F. Gordon, *A Gazetteer of the State of New Jersey ... Accompanied by a Map* (Trenton, NJ: Daniel Fenton, 1834), 104. We thank David Cohen for directing us to this source.

[6]At Jersey City, NJ, above Ellis Island.

[7]At Patterson, NJ.

eat Breakfast & took a Walk of abt. 1/2 Mile to the Falls, where we were very agreeably surpris'd to find a Scene far more romantic than any of us had ever seen a beautiful fall of abt. 40 feet wide pouring down a perpendicular craggy precipice at a most rapid Rate 67 feet in height, where dashing against the Rocks it roard prodigiously loud & emptied itself into a large Bason below, the high Mountains on every Side except where the Water Falls are compos'd of an amazing heap of Pebble Stones & are steep & dangerous as well as difficult to get up, the Water falling into between two perpendicular Rock which form'd a kind of Avenue, & a great Draft of Air constantly rising from the Mouth of the fork, the Water is blown up high into the Air all round the Falls & there is a continual Rain, & at 12 O Clock whenever the Sun shines we see a very pretty Rainbow — after viewing every thing about here we return'd to the Tavern to dine, when we set off another Road than what we had come for N York, the Road from Newark to the Falls as well as part of the Road back led along the bank of the Pasaick River & gave us many very pretty Prospects the Rivers smooth Surface with the Vessels sailing down & being remarkably strait made the Scene enterta[in]ing & agreeable & I do not recollect any Part of Pennsylvania or Maryland that where there is a prettier Ride — returnd home in the Eveng. after crossing several Ferrys wh. are worse kept up than any near Philadelphia & make the Rides about N York much less agreeable

25

This Morning wrote to several of my Friends breakfasted with R B: collected such Necessaries as were wanting for our Journey din'd at home with Company drank Tea at C:& S—s & spent the Evening at home —

26th

This Morning having provided all our Accomodations for the Tour we sent them on board the Sloop Royal George Capt. Walden with whom we had agreed to go to Albany having got an early Dinner we went on board accompanied by some our Frds. all this Afternoon we were in Co. with several other Vessels who were bound to the same Place. we set off with a fair tho a light Breeze & got up the River Hudson abt. 8 Mile when the whole Fleet were oblig'd to come to Anchor on Account of the Wind dying away & a strong tide ^of ebb^ against. This River runs ~~here~~ abt. N & S: except some pieces of high Land which project far out & alter its direction, its breadth is abt. 1/4 ^Mile^ — many Porpoises play betwixt us & the Shore — the N York Side was at first steep & high & afforded several pretty Situations for Gentlemans Seats, the West was more sloping & cover'd with Woods & here appear'd several Farm Houses surrounded with Fields of Grain — The Ground of which the steep Shores consisted was of a pale brick colour, or the Stones were of ~~were of~~ grey sand Stone, the high Hills on one Side cover'd with a continued Foliage except here & there a Valley where a little Farm house was seen & the sloping of the Banks on the other which were more improv'd & cover'd with every Species of Grain, the Silver stream which now enjoy'd a happy Calm offered a very picturesque & romantic View heighten'd by ^a^ fine ~~clear~~ serene Evening & the fleecy Clouds wh. we just saw peeping over the Tops of the Trees exhibited Scenes on every Side ~~equally~~ agreeable & delightful —

27.

Having weighd Anchor last Night, we came along with a head Wind abt. 10 Mile, anchor'd again abt. 5 this Morning the Wind however in abt. 3 hours freshen'g up we came along very slow which however was very pleasant, as we sail ~~along~~ within a few yards of the West Shore all this Distance the Rocks being excessive high & almost perpendicular they are cover'd with a greyish Moss except where peices have lately fallen from, which lay close to the Margin of the Water & appear at high Water like a regular Wharf built all the Distance the Cedar & other Trees grow thick from allmost every break in the Rock whch are very close to each other & they seem half cover'd with variegated Verdure, the Rocks on the Side we suppose to be at least 200 feet high & some of them almost project their heads over the River,[8] the other Side is equally beautiful the more natural the Trees growing sometimes in Clusters, ~~& sometimes~~ where they appear almost an impenetrable Forrest, & sometimes single on the [word crossed out] ^rising^ Plains, & the great variety of Grain which is now almost mature for Harvest in many Fields around, bedeck

---

[8]This section of the Hudson Valley has since been called the Palisades.

the Scene — [words crossed out] ^with Beauty & Variety^ having past
these we approach a Country beaut richly cultivated & improv'd for many
miles together the a Wide Level near the Water & then the ground began
to rise regular & even, on both sides of the River & further back a
verdant Crown of Woods which seem to rise as far as our Eyes could
extend, the Orchards growing in Fields of Corn & many of the Fences
thickly borderd with Trees on the Sloping Hills, the horses grazing on the
Medows & a regular Row of Trees growing along the Waters Edge found
a Scene very pleasing [word crossed out] passing this we came to a
Country which they call the high Lands the River here by the Projection
of successive Rocks on each Side the Shore is made very narrow in many
Places not wider than the Skuylkill [Schuykill River], the Hills seem to
grow out of the Water & trees appear half buried in it, wherever we see a
Dale which is not often near the Water Edge we see a little Cottage, in
these Places we fir'd several Guns, the Echoes of which reverberated like
Peals of Thunder & increas'd in Sound towards the last, after sailing abt.
15 Miles thro an Avenue of these Montrous Hills wch almost seeled us
from the Light of the Day we take leave of the last which is call'd Butter
hill.[9] This & one or two next it & those opposite exceeded any of the
rest, ^we suppose their height 700 feet perpendicular Proud & majestic^
the look was awful in some Places the rough rude Rock was bare but for
the most Part coverd with Trees which seem'd to have no Earth to feed
them during these 15 Mile We seem'd to be continually confin'd as to
prospect on the River, the jutting out of the Rock in so many Points kept
us continually as it were in a kind of Bason, & on the whole 'twas the
most romantic Scenes by far I ever saw — after we now bid adieu to
these majestic narrows, & come many miles thro Places thick settled &
cultivated, the ground gently rising as we look further on both Sides
appear'd alike, we sail by several very prettily situated Villages, Newburn
[Newburgh], Newberry,[10] Fishkill Landing[11] &c. which we reckon Sixty
Miles from New York, & a little beyond this we have a Reach up & down
the River abt. 12 Mile this too was an agreeable Prospect.

---

[9]This is Storm King Mountain on the west side of the Hudson River north of West Point. It was
called Butter Hill, a translation of the Dutch *Boterberg*, until the 1860s.
[10]Perhaps a mishearing and then duplication of Newburgh.
[11]Opposite Newburgh on the Hudson River.

28t

Having sail'd most part of the last Night we came to anchor before Day
about 80 Miles from Albany & weigh'd anchor early this Morning we
sail'd along thro a more settled Country than the Day before tho by
means those very beautiful & Romantic Prospects, we
were the greatest ^Part^ of the Day in Sight of the blue Mountains,[12] &
abt. 11 O Clock we were nearly opposite them & tho they seemd very
near us we were told they were 12 Miles distant, as we leave them further
off they appear like a thick black lowering Cloud in the Evening it fell
almost calm & we being in a long ^strait^ narrow part we had a Reach
which was open several Miles up & down the River it looked very
beautiful the Moon shining very bright we staid on Deck ^till^ late at
Night & ~~with~~ ^being^ little wind ~~& the moon shing very bright the~~
~~water &~~ all around ~~look~~ was very agreeable — abt. 12 O Clock we got up
to Albany came along Side the Wharf but did not come from onboard
[*Capt: Waldon behav'd to us with the greatest Politeness he is a civil obliging*
Man —]

29!

Cartwright[13] & after breakfast went to see the Cohoes Falls, which are
about 12 Mile from Albany, we undressd ourselves & measd. the Weadth
which we made 900 feet & in Height 75 — The Prospect from above
look [remainder of page torn off].

> Smooth to the shelving Brink a Copious Flood
> Rolls fair & placid when collected all [word illegible]
> In one impetuous torrent down the Steep
> In thundering shoots & shakes the Country round,
> As first an Azure sheet it rushes broad;
> Then whitening by degrees, as prone it falls
> And from the loud resounding Rocks below
> Dash'd in a Cloud of foam, it sends aloft

---

[12] The high peaks of the Catskill Mountains west of the Hudson Valley.
[13] Richard Cartwright (1720–94), the loyalist proprietor of one of Albany's most notable inns, "The King's Arms." Colonial Albany Social History Project; see <http://www.nysm.nysed.gov/albany/ bios/c/ ricartwright6508.html>.

Albany 1789

A hoary Mist & forms a ceaseless shower.
Nor can the tortured Wave here find repose
But raging still amid the Shaggy Rocks
Now flashes o'er the Scatter'd Fragments, now
Aslant the hollow Channel rapid darts
And falling fast from gradual Slope to Slope
With wild infracted Course, & lessened Roar,
It gains a safer Bed & steals at last
Along the mazes of the Quiet Vale — [14]

Albany is very advantageously situated on the North River[15] at the Head
of the tide abt. 160 Miles from N York, the Houses are in Number abt.
600 almost all built in the Dutch Taste the Gable Ends fronting the
Street, & wherever two Houses join as the Eves of the Roof will always

---

[14] Fisher, perhaps from memory, inserts an excerpt from "Summer," one of four poems that in 1793
were published together as *The Seasons*, the masterwork of the Scottish poet, James Thompson (1700–48).
"Summer," however, had been separately printed in 1727. See James Thompson, *The Seasons* (London:
T. Longman, B. Law and Son, etc., 1793), 109. Fisher's skills of recall are attested to in Anna Wharton
Smith, *Genealogy of the Fisher Family, 1682 to 1896* (Philadelphia, 1896), 34, who reports that, while
in England, he "was waited for with eagerness at one of the coffee-houses in London, because he could
repeat, almost verbatim, all the speeches of the preceding night in Parliament."

[15] For many decades the Hudson River was called the North River, the name given it by the Dutch
early in the seventeenth century, that is, *Noortrivier*.

touch each other there is a long Spout ~~comes~~ projects out of the Street [*There is a pretty considerable Fortification but it is now in Ruins from the Top of this there is the most perfect View of the Town — notwithstanding the excellent situation of the Place ^at the head of so fine a River^ for trade, so great Enemies are the Inhabitants to trade that till this kind of People are remov'd, or they (are) supplanted by one of a more enterpris.g Genius it will not cut much figure*][.] there is a very considerable Trade carried on here & a vast deal of Produce sent from hence to N York, as there are 40 Vessels who each carry equal to 500 Barlls constantly in the trade, the principal Articles are Wheat, Flour, Furrs Pot Ash, Bean, Staves, Tar, &c. there are a ~~good~~ ^small^ Number of Sea Vessels here — One Scow in the London [trade] which comes in 2 [i.e., twice] a year & brings considerable Quantities of dry Goods —

30th

Having yesterday settled upon going to the Falls of Niagara we spent this Morning in getting such things as were necessary for our Expedition, & agreed for a Waggon to take us to Schenectady & after dining with S: Delancey[16] to whom we were recommended by W.F of N York we set out in a very curious Waggon without cover or Seats & nothing but our Luggage & some Hay to keep us from the Bottom of the Waggon [*The Waggons of this Co. which are the only Carrge of Pleasure merit a Description they are 4 Weels with some Boards laid on with out any kind of Exactness with regard to Length & two Side Boards fix'd on. some of them have a Board behind them, which one might lean back ag.t did they not jar so, that it is done at the Expense of a soar back, tho to remedy which Inconveniency there a suffic.t Quat. of hay put in, as well as to keep one from jolting agt. the Bottom — there being no Seats all—*] & arriv'd at Schenectady abt. 8 O Clock in the Evening Schenectady is 16 Miles from Albany very pleasantly situated on the Mohawk River, inhabited most by low Dutch, the Land it stands on is very poor & sandy, as it is all the Way on the Road from Albany tho it is only a narrow Strip where there grow nothing but Pines & Aspin Trees,[17] yet there is on both Sides a very

---

[16]Probably Stephen De Lancey (1738–1809), attorney and then clerk of the city and county of Albany. Colonial Albany Social History Project; see <www.nysm.nysed.gov/albany/bios/d/stdl. html>.

[17]The area between Albany and Schenectady that Fisher describes is today called the Pine Bush. The name "Schenectady," a town established in the early 1660s, is derived from the Mohawk *skahnéhtati*, meaning "it is beyond the pines."

fine improv'd & thick settld Country, there are in Schenectady about 400 Houses & 3 Churches [and] ^a Fort^ The River runs so crooked that it almost surrounds it, a vast deal of fine Meadow & arable Ground in the Neighbourhood, & carries on a very considerable & profitable Trade with the Indians — [*without wh. indeed it could not subsist, there are several 100, Boats go from this Place to Niagara & some to Detroit loaded with Dry & Wet Goods this is the Place from whence all Boats set out that go to the Back Parts of the Province the River not being navigable but a very (few?) Miles lower down on acct. of the Cohoes Falls*]

July 1st

Having some Letters of Introduction to P: & Ellis[18] of this Place we called on them this Morning where we breakfasted, after which we took a Walk about the Town to view it. got the several Articles that were wanting to compleat our Preparation for the Rout, the Men being come from Albany to go with us, we got such things done to our Batteau [*which we calld the Amor Lovely*] as were necessary, & having received a kind Invitation from P & E: we dind with them — first seeing every thing put on board of the batteau [*Sent our Servt. with her —*] with Orders to proceed up the River to Thompsons[19] when we were to meet them, after Dinner took a Walk over the ~~creek~~ ^River with P & E^ where is a pretty situated Country Betterment the ground rich & fine, returnd with them in the Evening drank tea Supp'd —

2nd.

Rose at 4 got into the Waggon drove off for Col: Guy Johnsons Son in Law to Sr. Wm.[20] who havg had his house lately burnt down was not at

---

[18]The provisioning and fur trading company of [James] Phyn, [Alexander] Ellice, and Company, established in 1768. See R. H. Fleming, "Phyn, Ellice and Company." *Contributions to Canadian Economics* 4(1932): 7–41.

[19]Probably John Thompson, whose farm was within the bounds of Cosby's Manor, up the Mohawk river from German Flats, Herkimer County, NY. See Samuel Ludlow Frey, ed., *The Minute Book of the Committee of Safety of Tryon County* ... (New York: Dodd, Mead, 1905), 128; Harold C. Syrett, ed., *Papers of Alexander Hamilton*, vol. 19 (New York: Columbia University Press, 1973), 200.

[20]Sir William Johnson (1715–74), the celebrated Crown agent and superintendent of Indian affairs for the Northern Department. See Fintan O'Toole, *White Savage: William Johnson and the Invention of America* (Albany: State University of New York Press, 2009). Guy Johnson (b.c. 1740–88), nephew and deputy of Sir William Johnson, who replaced his uncle as superintendent of Indian affairs upon his death.

his own but at the house of Col: Closer, [*on the Mohawk River*]²¹ a Cousin of Col: Johnson,²² he was very obliging to us sorry his late Misfortune had deprivd ~~us~~ ^him^ the Pleasure of entertaining us at his own house & gave us some Instruction & Information relative to our Tour 11 O Clock sat out rode thro Fort Hunter a little Village where about 100 Indians reside who all live by ~~huntin~~ ^Farming^ having a large tract of Land prettily situated on a S:West Branch of the Mohawk²³ of which tribe the Indians here are ~~a tribe~~ They are very peaceable & industrious, [~~here is a School lately establish~~] have a School & Church the latter being under the Pastorship of Dr. Stuart²⁴ who is appointed by the Society for propogating the Gospel to preach ^to^ & baptise them, which several of them have been done hence to Johnstown where we din'd, after Dinner went to Johnson Hall [*which is pleasantly situated on a rising Ground abt. 1 Mile from Jntown*]²⁵ to see Sr. Wm. who behav'd to us with much Respect shew'd us all the Civilities in his Power, gave us Directions for our Procedure &c & supp'd & lodgd with him, he had then as is usual a good deal of Company. Johnstown is but a little ~~Town~~ ^Settlement^, being lately made the Capital of a County which is but just divided & settled, this is calld Tryon in honor of their present Governor²⁶ who is much belovd throughout the Province, the Lands here are very rich & well water'd tho not yet any very great Number of Settlements —

---

²¹Guy Johnson's home was destroyed sometime earlier in a fire caused by a lightning strike; Sir William Johnson, *Papers of Sir William Johnson*, 14 vols., eds. James Sullivan et al. (Albany: University of the State of New York, 1921–1962), 8:823.

²²The journal reads that "Closer" was "A cousin of Col: Johnson." However, this person is Christian Daniel Claus (1727–87), Sir William Johnson's son-in-law, who served as an interpreter and British Indian agent. See Helga Doblin and William A. Starna, eds. and trans., *The Journals of Christian Daniel Claus and Conrad Weiser: A Journal to Onondaga, 1750* (Philadelphia: American Philosophical Society, 1994).

²³Fort Hunter, and within, its palisade Queen Anne chapel, were built in 1711–12 and refurbished in 1755. The fort and the adjacent Mohawk village of Tiononderoge (var.), from the Mohawk *teyoñtaró:keñ*, meaning "junction of two waterways" or "between two waterways," were located at the mouth of Schoharie Creek. See Floyd G. Lounsbury, "Iroquois Place-Names in the Champlain Valley." In *Neighbors and Intruders: An Ethnohistorical Exploration of the Indians of Hudson's River*, eds. Laurence M. Hauptman and Jack Campisi (Canadian Ethnological Services, Paper 39. Ottawa: National Museum of Man, 1978), 108, 135. An Indian school was reported to be in operation at Fort Hunter in late 1770, and it may have continued so until just before the Revolution. John Wolfe Lydekker, *The Faithful Mohawks* (Port Washington: Ira J. Friedman, 1938), 128. On the Mohawk people, here and elsewhere in Fisher's journal, see William N. Fenton and Elisabeth Tooker, "Mohawk." In *Handbook of North American Indians*. Vol. 15, *Northeast*, ed. Bruce G. Trigger (Washington, DC: Smithsonian Institution, 1978), 466–80.

²⁴Rev. John Stuart (1740–1811) served at Fort Hunter from 1770 to 1777. A loyalist, he escaped into Canada in 1781, settling at Cadaraqui (Kingston, Ont.). See Lydekker, *Faithful Mohawks*.

²⁵Johnson Hall is today a State Historic Site and a National Historic Landmark.

²⁶William Tryon (1729–88) served as governor of New York from 1771 to 1780; see Paul David Nelson, *William Tryon and the Course of Empire: A Life in the British Imperial Service* (Chapel Hill: University of North Carolina Press, 1994).

3d

Breakfasted & took leave of Sir Wm. Johnson, came to the Tavern,
& sat off for Ca^a^nnewaga[27] staid a few Min: with Major Funda,[28] rode
thro a fine level Country altogether improv'd along the Mohawk River, on
both Sides of us high hill wc. were rather barren, or unimprov'd to [letter
crossed out] a Tavern near Anthonys Nose,[29] 4 O C where din'd, staid till
4 O Clock here under a pleasant shady Tree, when we set on & reach
Wm. Sebers[30] a Tavern on the other Side of the River, we pass'd a Hill abt.
2 Miles from Johnstown which is thought by many to afford the finest
Prospect in America, we look down a vastly deep Valley & see for a long
Course the River Mohawk running in beautiful Meanders thro a richly
cultivated continuance of Land for many Miles every Way ^[word
illegible]^ while we look above & see a vast succeeding Progression of
Mountains, contending with each other for height some all round at such
distances that they can scarcely be discernd from [word crossed out]
Clouds — the whole strike a Reverence & awe whc. cannot be possibly
describ'd —

4th

Sat off at 6 O Clock for Conojohary Castle an Indian Settlement abt. 20
Familys, breakfasted under a Tree on Sour Milk & Bread, & afterwards

---

[27] Caughnawaga, a locale just west of Fonda, NY, from the Mohawk *kahnawă·ke*, meaning "at the rapids." This was also the name of a Mohawk village there, occupied from about the 1680s until its abandonment and destruction by the French in 1693; Dean R. Snow, *Mohawk Valley Archaeology: The Sites*. The Institute for Archaeological Studies (Albany: University at Albany, State University of New York, 1995), 431–43.

[28] Jellis Fonda (1727–91), a prominent local resident and successful trader, entrepreneur, and land speculator, after whose father the village of Fonda was named. Jellis served as a major in the militia and commanded a company at the Battle of Oriskany in August 1777.

[29] Anthony's Nose is the name given to a precipitous hill on the north side of the Mohawk River at Yosts. Local histories mention that there was a tavern called Dockstader's at this place.

[30] William Seeber's tavern on Sand Hill, a short distance northwest of Fort Plain. Seeber was mortally wounded, and his son Audulph killed, at the Battle of Oriskany. A second son, Jacob, suffered a leg wound there and later died at Fort Herkimer; John Albert Scott, *Fort Stanwix (Fort Schuyler) and Oriskany* . . . (Rome: Rome Sentinel Company, 1927), 220.

went to a Church built on Purpose for the Indians[31] & where Dr. Stuart preaches the same as at Fort Hunter the Number of Indians who attended were abt. 60, they behav'd with the greatest Decency & Respect, for the Purpose they were assembled appear'd devout, & joind Prayer, sung Psalms with great Propriety — these too are of the Mohawk Tribe & are well spoken of by the whites, they have in the late Warr been strongly attach'd to the English Interest, after Church rode abt. 2 Mile to Dygarts[32] where we din'd, set off & reach Thompsons[33] abt. 6 O Clock, here we found our Batteau Men. there were 150 Indians of the Oneyda [Oneida] Tribe who had come from several Settlements to lay a State of their present Situation before Sir Wm. J—n & to beg of him such Assistance as their Case requir'd they being in absolute Want of Provisions for Support, their Lands being newly improvd & Harvest not yet come on, as their Zeal had been great for the Interest of the whites, they had no Doubt of receiving such necessary Supplies, as were immediately necessary, they behavd very kind to us had built themselves many Wigwams,[34] but they ^could^ not talk English — Lodged here this Evening & on the

---

[31] "Conojohary Castle," a multiethnic Indian community composed primarily of Mohawks, was also known as Dakanohage (var.), Canajoharie, Fort Canajoharie, and Fort Hendrick. Occupied from about 1700 to 1777, the settlement consisted of dwellings lying between East Canada Creek and the mouth of Nowadaga Creek, three miles east of Little Falls. The church, built as an Anglican chapel at the urging of Sir William Johnson in 1769, and located just east of Nowadaga Creek, is on the National Register of Historic Places; see Snow, *Mohawk Valley Archaeology*, 485–93; Philip Lord, Jr., "Taverns, Forts, and Castles: Rediscovering Hendrick's Village." *Northeast Anthropology* 52 (1996): 69–94; "Indian Castle Church," <http://indiancastle.com/ICNHL.htm>. Canajoharie is from the Mohawk *kana'tysyóhare*, meaning "washed kettle," a name applied to an earlier village at Fort Plain. Lounsbury, *Iroquois Place-Names*, 108.

[32] The "late Warr" was the French and Indian War (1754–63). Here, Warner Dygert (b. 1719), a farmer and innkeeper of Palatine German descent living on Fall Hill, south of Little Falls, where in 1780 he reportedly was killed by Indians. See William V. H. Barker, *Early Families of Herkimer County, New York* (Baltimore: Genealogical Publishing, 1986), 66.

[33] See note 26.

[34] Fisher is using "wigwam," a word derived from southern New England Algonquian, as a generic for any Indian dwelling he happened to see. The Oneidas and other Iroquoians of the period, as did many New England natives, commonly lived in rectangular, pole-framed, bark-covered houses or cabins, and also log homes. On the Oneida people, here and elsewhere in Fisher's journal, see Jack Campisi, "Oneida." In *Handbook of North American Indians*. Vol. 15, *Northeast*, ed. Bruce G. Trigger (Washington, DC: Smithsonian Institution, 1978), 481–90. See also Alan Taylor, *The Divided Ground: Indians, Settlers, and the Northern Borderland of the American Revolution* (New York: Alfred A. Knopf, 2006); Karim M. Tiro, *The People of the Standing Stone: The Oneida Nation from the Revolution Through the Era of Removal* (Amherst: University of Massachusetts Press, 2011).

5th.

Early in the morning we embarked on board our Batteau paddled off against the Stream & about 10 Miles distant we landed, made a fire sent to a house some Distance for Milk, this with some Bread & Butter we made a hearty breakfast of, boild the remainder of our Milk to take along with us, from this we went along the River abt. 5 Miles, where we went on Shore made a Fire & fry'd some Gammon & Eggs of which made a hearty Dinner from hence 9 Miles where we went on Shore, cut down Several Trees, mov'd away the Nettles & Grass which grew with uncommon Rampancy, made a Fire, pitchd our Tent, & hav.g shot a couple of Pidgeons, we boild them with Gammon &c. & made some excellent Broth of which we supp'd heartily & making a Large Fire on every Side we were pretty ^free^ from Musquitos & Knats, made up our Bed, & never rested better nor more comfortable —

6th

Rose this Morning at 5. packd up our all, put them on board & again set forward, after com.g 6 Mile up the River we breakfasted on Milk & bread & butter here we landed & walk up the Rest of the Way (abt. 3 Mile) to Fort Stannix,[35] Din'd here & went to look abt. the Place as this is the last Settlement we are to find all the Way till we come to Oswego, we got what other Provisions we thought necessary, sent them on board — there is at this Place a Carrying Place of abt. 1 M. from Mohawk to Wood Creek[36] our Batteau &c. was here carried across, & not being Water enough in Wood Creek we are detained here this After till the Water in a Lake which feeds the Creek rises for whc. Purpose there is a Flood Gate & as it is now a very dry Season & the Water very ^low^ it takes more time than usual to get a Quantity of Water sufficient to float our

---

[35]Fort Stanwix, at present-day Rome, NY, was completed about 1762. Abandoned by the British in 1774, it was reoccupied by American troops two years later and renamed Fort Schuyler. It burned to the ground in 1781. Two of the most important treaties between the Iroquois nations, the first in 1768 with the British, and the second in 1784 with the Americans, took place here. See Jack Campisi, "From Stanwix to Canandaigua: National Policy, States' Rights, and Indian Land." In *Iroquois Land Claims*, eds. Christopher Vecsey and William A. Starna, 49–65 (Syracuse: Syracuse University Press, 1988).

[36]An important portage, one to six miles in length depending on the time of year, from the head of Wood Creek, west of Fort Stanwix, to the head of the Mohawk River to its east.

Bark — A Barber ~~here~~ being sent for to shave us, a woman appeard who perform'd the Operation with great Skill & Dexterity — After Dinner Some Ottowaw [Ottawa] Indians[37] hearing there were some Gentlemen in the next House who were on their Travels to Niagara &c waited on us, & after some Conversation by means of an Interpreter they presented us with the Head & Neck of a Deer they had just before Kill'd. this Part of the Deer it seems is the most honorable Present they are capable of makg among these Indian was one of their Chiefs, they had left their Wives & Families abt. 1 Mile from Fort Stannix at the Landing on the Mohawk they were on a visit to Sir William Johnson whom they annually go to see, to carry Presents & to renew their old Treaty of Union & assure him of the inviolable Regard they yet retain for the English — we gave them 2 Glasses of Rum each, abt. which not being content they informd us, that Sir William never let them go without a Bottle, which we thought it best to give them & also some Buiscuit when they went away thankful for what they had receivd & bad[e] us farewell —

7th

By Sunrise this Morning we were knock'd up by [letter crossed out] one of the Indians who had honor'd us wth. a Visit the Night before, & who now came to present us with some smoak'd Eels & beg of us some more bread, & on our inform.g him that the Batteau in which our Bread was, had gone forwd. & that we could not get at the Bread, he order'd his Son to take away the Eels he had brought us which he accordingly without much Ceremony did, after this we went down to the Place they had built their Wigwams & bid them all farewel. This we did least they shd. think proper to call on us, after this we returnd, eat Breakfast & sat out on Foot from the Fort hav.g ~~before~~ sent the Boat down before us abt. 8 Mile, which we thought most prudent to do as ~~Wood~~ ^Kennedy^ Creek was very crookd & shallow & the Distance by Land only 4 Mile, we reach'd the Place abt. 9 O Clock & waited there till abt. 12. when the Boat came down here we din'd & sat off abt. 1 thro a very crooked narrow shallow River, & got abt. 8 Miles below, when we pitchd our Tent, & eat a Suppr hav.g a Wood Cock, Duck, & Pidgeon which we shot, also a Chicken & some Venison Beef & Ham of all which we made a very dilicious Repast.

---

[37] The Ottawas, an Algonquian-speaking people whose homeland was the Michigan Lower Peninsula and environs.

8th

At 6 O Clock this Morning we sat off to proceed on our Journey much
plagued with the Musquitos as we had been the Night before, got abt. 4
Mile down when we came to & breakfasted, push'd forward & got 12
Mile further down to dine, being at the Mouth of Wood Creek which
opens into Oneyda Lake & commands a very extensive & pretty Prospect,
the first 26 Mile coming down Wood Creek is very narrow & shallow, the
land very Rich & Level but so inhabited by the Tribes of Muskitos &
Mitches [midges] that it is very disagreeable & uncomfortable, after
Dinner sat off with a Head Wind, made but little Way for some time
when it fell calm & we progressd on tolerably, The R̶i̶v̶ Lake being calm,
[*On the No. Side of this Lake live the Tuscarora Indians who are rather
troublesome the South & other Sides are inhabited by the Oneydas*][38] & the
Blue Mountains[39] appearing at a great Distance & very high over the
Trees on the Margin of the Lake, look very pretty, we came to abt. 11
Mile from the beggin'g of the Lake where we enchamp & hav.g killd
some Bullfrogs & a Pheasant we pleasantly regald ourselves on the Fruits
of [letters crossed out] our Labour, but Night coming on apace, & with it
such a Number of Muskitos that almost darken'd the Skies, we attempted
to invoke Morpheus to reign among ^us^, & hav.g in vain try'd for many
hours, but finding the little Animals so numerous, & so watchful, as well
as intolerably noisy we concluded to sat off again which we did abt. 1 O
Clock in the Morning of the

9th

& partly sailing & partly row.g we got into Onondago [Onondaga]
^River^[40] [*a little back of this* h̶e̶r̶e̶ *resides the Onondago Indians*] by 5 O
Clock which was 21 Mile & coming by an Indian Eel Ware [weir], where

---

[38]Historical sources have the Tuscaroras living generally south of Oneida Lake at this time, the
Oneidas south of the east end of the lake. See David Landy, "Tuscarora Among the Iroquois." In *Handbook
of North American Indians*. Vol. 15, *Northeast*, ed. Bruce G. Trigger (Washington, DC: Smithsonian
Institution, 1978), 520; Campisi, "Oneida," 481.

[39]The foothills of the Adirondack Mountains.

[40]Today it is called the Oswego River. At the outbreak of the Revolution, most of the Onondagas
were residing in their homeland between Onondaga Creek and Cazenovia Lake. On the Onondaga people,
see Harold Blau, Jack Campisi, and Elisabeth Tooker, "Onondaga." In *Handbook of North American Indians*.
Vol. 15, *Northeast*, ed. Bruce G. Trigger (Washington, DC: Smithsonian Institution, 1978), 491–99.

the Indians resort in the Summer Months to catch Eels & smoake them which last all the year. There were here near an hundred Indians of the Onondago tribe, we stopd & barter'd some of our Buiscuit for their Eels giving one for one, we breakfasted abt. a Mile below this, & row'd down the River to the Place the Seneca Onondago & Oswego Rivers join each other [*here reside the Seneca's who are thought to be the most active active (sic) & the greatest Warriors of all the 6 Nations*][41] where we came ashore but being pursu'd by some Indians we thought it most prudent to fix on some other Spot, & came about a Mile lower down where we din'd & bath'd & were here visited by some Indians who behaving well we gave each of them a Buiscuit & some Rum, came by another Indian Eel Ware, where there was an equal Number but we had no Connections with them abt. 4 O Clock we came by the Oswego Falls where we were oblig'd to get out & unload the Boat & carry our Goods & her abt. 35 feet over the Land, these Falls are abt. 9 feet perpendicular height, & 600 Wide they are very rapid above & below, & their appearance is romantic, here was formerly a Fort & considerable Fortifications,[42] but they are now destroy'd, we came down about 2 Miles below, & enchamp'd on a little rising Ground the Mitches were here, more troublesome than Muskitos but having been the Night before without ~~Sleep~~ ^Repose^ we the More readily fell into a sound sleep —

10th

Rose at 5 Set off & came all the Way down the Rapids to Oswego Fort,[43] breakfasted ~~at~~ on the Beach below the Fort at the Mouth of Oswego River where it empties itself into the Lake of Ontario, ~~where~~ we came all the Way from Fort Stannix to this Place with the Stream — Stannix is at the head of Wood Creek abt. 1/2 a Mile from the head of the Mohawk River, & is ~~thought to be the highest~~ Land in America ^to No. & East.d^

---

[41]By the mid-eighteenth century, the Senecas were settled at the south ends of Canandaigua and Seneca Lakes and down the Chemung River. Others were along the Genesee River. On the Seneca people, see Thomas S. Abler and Elisabeth Tooker, "Seneca." In *Handbook of North American Indians*. Vol. 15, *Northeast*, ed. Bruce G. Trigger (Washington, DC: Smithsonian Institution, 1978), 505–17.

[42]This was the Oswego Falls Palisade, also called Fort Bradstreet, built in 1758–59 at what is today the village of Fulton.

[43]Fisher actually saw Fort Ontario, erected on the east bank of the Oswego River in 1755 and rebuilt in 1759 after it was destroyed, along with Fort Oswego (a.k.a. Fort Pepperill and Fort George) on the west bank, by a large French force under the command of General Louis-Joseph de Montcalm in 1756.

as the Waters run down to every Quarter from it, on one Side the
Mohawk River, which has a great Number of Falls & Drifts this empties
itself into Hudsons River above the Tide, on the other Side is Wood
Creek, where there is a gentle Stream into Oneyda Lake, which runs into
Onondaga River, into which Seneca empties itself, & this & Seneca then
come into Oswega when the River widens Considerably, Oswego
emptying itself by many Falls & Rapids into Ontario & Ontario runs into
St. Lawrence, as the Fall from Fort Stannix to Oswego is computed at 250
feet, & the fall of Lake Erie into Ontario is only it must be higher than
Erie, which is as high as the first Waters of Ohio which empty themselves
into the Mississipy after Breakfast we went up to view the Fort which
stands on a pretty Eminence & overlooks the Surf which as the Wind is
now high at West roars considerably the Fort is built of Wood, but is now
decaying fast there are 2 White Families here, which is the ^only^
Settlement except of Indians all the way between this & Fort Stannix
din'd on the Beach [*Wash'd our dirty Cloaths in the Lake*] & after Dinner
receiv'd an Invitation from Capt: sanford who commands a Sloop trading
from Niagara to Oswegochy [Oswegatchie][44] & This place ^to drink a
Dish of Tea with him^ which we accepted he afterwards came over the
River ^[word illegible]^ from where his Vessel lay & suppd with us on
some Bass wth wch. this Lake abounds — it began to rain we pitchd our
Tent on the Shore &c it being quite tight the Water could not get in, &
as it blew very hard, we had the Pleasure of being depriv'd of the Co. of
the Muskitos & Mitches —

11th

We were call'd up by Some Sailors who came from Capt. Sandford wt. an
Invitation to breakfast with him, we got up & went over the River —
took a Walk abt. 2 or 3 Mile along the Surf, which was very high, This
Shore is for the most part compos'd of greyish Rocks, which are nearly
flat & afford a pretty Walk the a little Way from the Water is thrown up
vast Quantities of pebble Stones of all Colors & Sizes very regular &
pretty we return'd With the Capt who din'd with us, after Dinner we took
a Walk along the Eastern Beach to a Place calld the 4 Mile Point[45] this

---

[44]Present-day Ogdensburg, NY.
[45]Described in local histories as a small head of land on the lake east of Oswego.

Walk was very tiresome as it was Stony most of the Way, in some few places Sandy & every here & there large Quantities of the ^best^ Black Sand, at this Place is a Creek which the ingenious Beavers have rais'd a Dam across ~~in this Place~~ as the Creek is large & a Number have resided many Years, in spight of the Hunters who have often attempted to catch them, in the Winter Season which is the only time as they can then walk on the Ice & go up to their houses, the hunters have never been able to catch above 2 or 3 in the Year — after brakf &c. we returnd to our Tent, & the Wind still continuing strong a head, we supp'd on some Partriges the Indians had brought us [& bath'd] & went to Bed — at this Place we heard of seven Prisoners the Onondago Indians had taken from the Chactaw [Choctaw] Nations, had them now in their Fort & had appointed the 10th of next month for roasting them & had sent Messengers to the several Nations to invite them to the Dance & to partake of the delicious Banquet —[46]

12th

We were call'd up this ~~Aft~~ Morn.g early with the agreeable Intelligence of a fair Wind, we immediately got every thing on board & set off with a NE wind, it blowing hard made a high Sea in the Lake, row'd abt. a Mile out when we hoisted our Sail & went away abt. 6 Mile an hour, but the Wind raising & gett.g more Northerly we were oblig'd to come to at 15 Miles distance from Oswego in a little Bay or Lak wh. made into Ontario, the Wind continuing to blow we pitch'd our Tent & breakfasted. in the Morning we walk'd round abt. the Bay, & after Dinner set out with our Boat, in quest of Birds & Fish, after going all round the Lake (wh. is

---

[46]This brief mention suggests that the Onondagas intended to torture and execute their captives, on whose remains they would feast. This follows a time-honored practice of Iroquoians that continued, although reports become increasingly infrequent, through the French and Indian War (Seven Years' War) and into the Revolution. See Nathaniel Knowles, "The Torture of Captives by the Indians of Eastern North America." *Proceedings of the American Philosophical Society* 82, no. 2 (1940): 211; Franklin B. Hough, ed. and trans., *Memoir Upon the Late War Between the French and English, 1755-1760 . . . by M.—Pouchot*, vol. 2 (Roxbury: W. Elliot Woodward, 186), 2:252; Frederick Cook, *Journals of the Military Expedition of Major John Sullivan Against the Six Nations of Indians in 1779 with Records of Centennial Celebrations* (Auburn: Knapp, Peck, and Thomson, 1887), 91. It might also have been the case that these Indians were posturing or exaggerating in an attempt to impress or frighten Fisher and his party. For an excellent analysis of the colonial-sourced propaganda that played up Indian cruelties on the frontier, see Peter Silver, *Our Savage Neighbors How Indian War Transformed Early America* (New York: W. W. Norton, 2008).

calld little Sodus)[47] we got sufficient of the Sea Bass Fish & Snipe to make a hearty & comfortable Supper, the Wind now falling & the Lake growing smooth we concluded best to set off that Evening & accordingly put every thing in our Boat, & by assisting the Men to row we progressed on abt. 24 Miles by 2 O Clock in the Mg when we just lay our Matrasses on the Beach & throwing the tent over us, we slept till Sunrise on the

13th

Again sat off got abt. 6 Mile to breakfast, after which the Wind freshen'd up & being fair we rig'd out our Sails, & running leisurely on abt. 4 Mile an hour, we thought best not to go ashore for our Din'r so we set to work on our Corps de Reserve wh. consisted of Ham & Peas on which we din'd heartily, abt. 4 O Clock this Afternoon we came by the Mouth of Jenusa [Genesee] River on which there are 2 Falls one of them 5 the other 7 Miles up the River but as we saw a good many of the Seneca Indians on the Beach & had heard they had committed several Insults on the Whites, we did not think it safe to venture up to see them which we otherwise intended we had pass'd them abt. 1 Mile when a Canoe with 5 of them in pursued & overtook us, they had caught some fish & having an Inclination to barter with us, we gave them some Bread, Rum, Shot & Tobacco on which they presented us with some large Cat Fish, & seeing our Number was greater than theirs they behav'd very civily, & saw meet to take leave of us, it being a Maxim among them, that it is always honorable for a Lesser to run from a greater Number, we push'd on & arriv'd at a Place call'd Braddocks Bay[48] [five lines crossed out] here we enchamp'd & supp'd on the Fish we had got of the Indians & went to Bed — the Muskitos were pleas'd to visit us, & in Spight of Tobacco & Smoak they took Possession of our Tent, & oppos'd our exculpatg them very formidably — 40 Miles this Day

14th

Rose this Morning abt. 3 O Clock got abt. 1 Mile on when it began to rain, but it soon cleard up & we reach'd 12 Miles to breakfast it now came on to blow fresh so that we could not leave the Place

---

[47]Little Sodus Bay, at Fair Haven, approximately fifteen miles west of Oswego.
[48]Braddock Bay, a short distance west of Rochester on Lake Ontario.

on Acct. of the high Sea till 11 O Clock ^when we^ again sat off & got 7 Miles further to Dinner — after which progress'd on, & got enchamp'd at the Mouth of a Creek 40 Miles from Niagara[49] we agree'd to rise early the next Morning by which we expected to reach our Port the next day — accordingly

July 15th

We rose between 12 & 1 O Clock the Lake calm as a Mill pond tho we heard it roar at a great Distance, which is a certain Prognostic that a Gale of Wind is at hand, our Men however row'd on & we got 12 Miles by Day Light, the Roaring of the Lake is heard more plain & we now have a pretty high Swell, we got a few Miles further on to Breakfast, & put on immediately after, but the Swell increasing & the wind rising & our Batteau not being able to [word illegible] we were oblig'd to put into a the 18 Mile Creek, we waited here till Dinner, & the Wind still continuing we concluded to walk up to Niagara & at 4 O Clock set off the Distance by Land 20 Miles, there being no Road we were oblig'd to take ^the^ Beach, which we found tiresome & fatiguing as it is either Sandy or Stony which was very Disagreeable our Feet continually slipping back at every Step, sometimes indeed we took into the Woods where there was no Path but here the Muskitos attack'd us with such Vigor, that we could scarce discern the exact Color of our Habits — by Industry Patience & Fatigue we however abt. 9 O Clock reach'd our Goal, & to our great Pleasure we found we had got into a Place where is almost every Luxury of Life, we at a short Notice were provided with a genteel Supper & Sleep being very desirable we went to bed this Day we got 40 Mile as we did each 24 hours during our Passage the Distance 160 M we made in 4 Days, which considering we had not one hour fair wind & were detain'd often by contrary winds, is a short Passage — indeed our whole Rout from Fort Stannix is short for the Season of the Year. the Springs which supply the Creeks being almost dried up, we have lodg'd in our Tents 9 Night & never have found the least Inconvenience except from the Muskitos, our marooning for ourselves was by no means disagreeable a considerable Part of our Provisions we shot ourselves they were all well cook'd & the great variety of Prospects we daily saw

---

[49]Possibly Oak Orchard Creek at Point Breeze, some thirty-five miles west of Braddock Bay.

render'd it an agreeable Ora, especially down the several Creeks, where was a continued Succession of pleasg Scenes, the Lake notwithstand.g much sameness in the Banks was pleasant. The water being so clear we could see the Bottom at some Fathoms Depth, & the repeated Bays & Points & Creeks serv'd for New Scenes to delight us, & our Batteau Men having behav'd very well, the whole has been a pleasant & agreeable time —

July 16th

After Breakfast this Morning we gave our Land Lord (Pollard)[50] Notice to procure us some horses ^to go to the Falls,^ we then waited on Col: Smith,[51] who resides within the Fort,[52] he gave us an Invitation to dine with ^him^ but as we were going to the Falls he excus'd us, he gave us Liberty to take the Kings Interpreter with us [*who understands 15 different Indn. Langu.*], as well for a Guide as to confer with any Indians we might chuse to converse with, we then waited on McClean[53] the Kings Commissary who we found much indispos'd or he would otherwise have waited on us to the Falls we then went to Phister[54] the Engineer, who was polite enough to give us Letter to Stedman[55] whose house is situated near the Falls; having got an early Dinner & our horses waiting at Door being sent us by the military Gentlemen of the Fort we mounted at 2 O Clock & sat out, & rode along Niagara River which is abt. 3/4 Mile wide the Banks very high & good Water remarkably green, which we overlook from the Sides at 9 Miles Distance there is the Landing Place, where all Boats going up are dischargd & the Goods carted across 9 Mile the River not being navigable any further up till above the Falls on account of the great Rapidity of the Water, here is a Capstain &c. to hall up the Goods

---

[50]This may be Edward Pollard, the proprietor of a sutler firm at Fort Niagara. See Calloway, "Fort Niagara," 134.

[51]Probably Lt. Col. Francis Smith (1723–91), 10th Regiment of Foot.

[52]Fort Niagara, on the east side of the Niagara River at its mouth on Lake Ontario, near Youngstown, N.Y.

[53]Deputy Commissary Neil McLean.

[54]Lt. Francis Pfister, a German-born engineer of the British 60th (Royal American) Regiment, held rights to the carrying place at Niagara. Over his career he produced several important manuscript maps of New York Colony and the adjacent region. Pfister, a loyalist, would lose his life in the battle of Bennington, Vermont, in August 1777.

[55]John Stedman, from England, settled in the Niagara Falls area about 1760 and involved himself in various enterprises on the portage route that passed around the falls. He later returned to his home country where he died in 1808.

to the Top of the Hill a Large & convenient Wharf for the Landing of them [letter crossed out] & Logs laid all the way along for Laying the Batteaus on — we waited here a little while, again sat off & abt. 5 reachd the house of Stedman which is a Mile & half from the Falls, we drank a Dish of Tea with him, & after this we went to view the Falls from the East Side of the River, From the Accounts I had read of the Grandeur of its Appearance I was induced to form Ideas of the Scene, which I was almost affraid would equal the Original, but here I felt how impossible it is to convey ~~Descriptions~~ ^Ideas^ of a Scene grand, magnificent & stupendous beyond all Description, the Falls from where we stood is 1/4 Mile wide to an Island call'd Stedmans [*the Island is near 1 Mile & the falls on the other Side of it tho by no means seen to the greatest Advantage is beautiful*],[56] the water over the Brow of the Fall is deep, it falls directly perpendicular 137 feet the roaring is immensely loud the Prospect of the Rapids from the Falls upward, is beautiful, to look below is majestic, & almost made me dizzy with the Sight, the Vapours rising below with the clashing of the Water rises high up in the Air & the Sun being near the West horrizon every Particle of Water from one particular Point of View appear'd like so many Diamonds floating in the Air whose supreminac Brilliancy dazzld my Eyes, here I could & here I should have staid till Darkness eclips'd my Sight, but being told [word crossed out] the other Side was still more grand, we fix'd on going there the next Morning, & after going half the Way down the Banks on wc. we stood, suspending our Selves by Roots &c. of Trees, or Stones some of which were loose, & the Fall of [word crossed out] ^one Stone or the Breaking of one Root either^ would in a Moment have deprived one of Existence, yet so great was my Curiosity to catch every View, that I gave no Room to reflect on the Danger of my Situation till casting my Eyes from the Waterfall to the Spot Under me I shudder'd at the View, took time to recollect & went up again astonishd tho not displeased at my Presumption, with Reluctance we now bid Adieu to the Scene till Morning — we went to the House of S: Where a very elegant & gentele Supper was provided for us, & very commodious Lodgings —

---

[56] Also called Goat Island, where Stedman was said to have kept a herd of goats.

Niagara Falls 1777

17th

Eager & impatient for the Sight of what we had came so far to see, rose early this Morning our hospitable Landlady suspecting our Situations got an early Breakfast for ~~but I~~ ^us^ & had put up ^the^ Corn Wine & Oil for our Regalement on the Jaunt, & the Landlord had provided us with

Batteaus & his own Men, to take across the River, & accompanied by his Partner Duffin,[57] we at 6 O Clock sat out, the Morning was calm, the Air was clear, the Sky was perfectly serene, on our getting a little Way out we had an open Prospect down the River Water perfectly [word crossed out] ^smooth^ for near a mile then rough, white, impetuous, rapid, while from the ~~Cle~~ Falls we see a ~~Succession~~ Cloud ~~successively~~ ^continually^ Ascending, rising swiftly, till it gaind a considerable height when the Wind carried it off ^a perfect compact cloud^ in a long succeeding Train, till it mingles with other Clouds this Cloud often serves for a Land— Mark to the Navigators in Ontario & Erie Lakes [*Col Smith informs us he had seen it (from) 45 mile(s)*] the River is here two Mile wide a Number of little Islands are seen on every Side of us, whose Verdure gives a pleasing View — we reach the further & have now 4 Mile to walk thro a thick & almost innaccessible Wood before we reach the important Spot Impatience however wing'd our Flight & in an hour we reach'd a ^flat^ Rock which is level with the Rocks from which the Water ~~the Water~~ ^falls its^ falling in many different Directions make an almost ^semi^ circular form, ^nearly^ in the Shape of a horse Shoe, & here it is seen to every Advantage, there are here three distinct separate Views of the Western Falls besides a full, front View of the Eastern. The Island abt. 400 y'ds in Width dividing them the lofty trees on the Top of which rather projecting over have a happy Effect in producing Variety — Here we see the ^whole^ collected Mass of Water [*170 Height 3/4 (mile) wide*] falling from the Stupendous Rocks like an amazing Sheet of melted Lead at first green but by Degrees ~~whit~~ lightening till at last it acquires a Whitness equal to Snow — the Mist near the bottom being so thick we cannot ~~hear~~ see the Water below — the Precipes on every Side the vast Stones continually falling down terrify beyond Imagination while the Grandeur the Magnificent the Beauty, wild irregularity & Romanticy of the Water steal the Soul from itself & charm it into Rapture — every thing round one is grand, & man dwindles to a Particle little more than an Atom — the Water 200 yards from the fall is so agitated ~~with~~ that ~~there~~ Surf there remains unappeas'd & the Waves run astonishingly high, after this it rushes forwards impeded in some Places by Rocks & Shallows which serve best the more to irritate it & render it a still confus'd unsettled

---

[57]A partner in the sutler firm of Duffin and Taylor at Fort Niagara. See Colin G.Calloway, "Fort Niagara: The Politics of Hunger in a Refugee Community." In *The American Revolution in Indian Country: Crisis and Diversity in Native American Communities* (Cambridge: Cambridge University Press, 1995), 134.

^misty^ Element of Water & Air — We were here alarm'd with a Wolf wch. we found watching for Prey as ~~it can~~ it frequently happens that Fowl swimming in the River above get hurl'd into the Rapids & finding it impossible to rise, the Water going like an Arow out of a Bow they are carried with the Stream into the flood below — this too is often the Case wh. Deer & other Beasts who in drinking are lifted off their Feet & become Food for the Beasts of Prey below. In our Walk among the Shrubs we met with several Rattle Snakes but fortunately escaptd being hurt by them — After this went along the ~~Hills~~ ^Banks^ abt. for a convenient Place, to go down the Mountains, after com'g this Distance we found the Way dangerous & dreadful, a Determination however to surmount all possible Difficulties to see the Whole embolden'd us, we went down the Place [*I saw a wolf here*], & all happily arriv'd there safe, then travell'd along over the Stones & Sands & Precipes sometimes creeping under Crags which nothing but unwarrantable Curiosity would have induc'd we got to ~~the~~ near the Falls & ~~that~~ the Spray wetting us, we were oblig'd to strip, when fearless of Danger we progress'd quite under the Rocks, & the Water with the utmost, rage immaginable insomuch that we were totalv blind ~~& then with~~ but not till we found ourselves nearly suffocated did we retire, wet as if we had been under Water, not so far up as this is a [letter crossed out] perpetual Shower, nothing can be more magnificent than the Rainbow which appears a little further of as we retire, & to look above & view the horrors of the Rocks which project far over us, & the Stones which perpetually fall down renders the Idea dreadful beyond Description after staying here 5 hours view.g every thing that was curious, we return'd fill'd with Astonishment at the Scene, which Words are too feeble to represent, & which an Idea heightend by any Picture that may be drawn will fall short of conceiving. indeed the horrors & Beauties of the Scenes blended exhibit Objects ~~fill'd~~ which fill one with awe & Astonishment — we now bid a long & sad Adieu to ~~the whole~~ every Object & this prompted by much less inviting Views than we went down, we ascended the hill more easily, & after attaining the height, we sat down by a cool running Stream slak'd our thirst with the good things our Landlady had given us & with some Bread & Cheese agreeably regal'd ourselves, we push'd on to ~~the~~ Stedmans which we reach 4 O Clock where the Table with a Dinner which would have done Credit to the first Philadelphia Table, hav'g undergone much ^fatigue^ we eat hearty went to see some Indians who had come a considerable Distance with considerable Quantity of Peltry, among them was Ausquijoon the ~~King~~

^greatest Warrior^ of all the five Nations, he is tall, strong, active
~~serious~~ & as likely a man as I have seen among the Indians he is
remarkably grave & serious a great Warrior & a great Politician — he
had an Invitation to spend the Evening with us he came, his Dress was
clean & elegant, he was affable & his Remarks were sensible & judicious,
his behaviour was graceful, modest, & genteel, he is thought to be proud
but it did not appear here, he is a ~~great Warrior~~ a Man of great ^spirit^ &
whose Looks when fir'd are fierce & furious, he is different from all other
Indians, in some particulars, [*he behav'd to us in particular as such as his
Wife (who is an English Woman & very pretty) with the greatest Politeness
shewd every man of Respect*] he is not willing to receive Presents; he
carries on trade not from Necessity but to lay up Money, he has a great
turn for farming, & is cultivating large tracts, & talks of building a Grist
Mill — Stedman our Landlord is much esteem'd by the Indians, to them
as to all Strangers he is very hospitable & generous, he has a Contract
with the King for carrying from the Landing Place I have describ'd to one
at his own house all the Provisions for the Use of the Forts Niagara &
Erie,[58] he has a Salary for this & all his horses are found at the Kings
Expence, with these & his Waggons he carries all the Furrs & Battows
that go & come to & from Detroit to Schenectady for each of wh. he has
£10 — which he can do in 2 Days with one Waggon tho he generally has
2 or 3 at Work his Station is thought to be worth at least †1800 clear of
every Charge & Expense —

18th

Having last Night fix'd on going to Fort Erie we rose early this
Morning & Stedman having provided us his Men & Battow to take us
there first drinkg some Milk Punch & eating some Bread we went on
board & the Stream being strong against us, our Progress was slow were
however well entertained with the Beauty of the River in going up [*The
Banks of the River are low & level the Bottom mostly sandy in some Places
Rocky*][.] It is in some Places 1 in others 2 in others 3 Miles Wide a
Number of large & smaller islands are pleasantly situated when we had
got abt. half Way up we met a Boat whereon was Capt: Mitham of 10th

---

[58]Built in 1764, Fort Erie was directly across the Niagara River from today's city of Buffalo. It served
as a supply base for British troops and loyalist militias.

Regt. who having heard of our coming, immediately got into our Boat & turn'd back to accompany us. his Conversation was very entertaining, he is a Man of Letters & the Gentleman, as soon as we landed we was a Mile from Fort Erie. we went up to his tent (his Apartment being now repairing) wh. was large & commodious, he very soon got us a genteel Dinner & shew'd us every Mark of Civility & Respect there, & after Dinner took us to view the Fort &c. which is small but the greatest Order & Regularity among the People, & is well adapted as a terrorim [?] for the Indians, which is very necessary, after this we went on board the Kings Schooner which carries 18 Guns, on our leaving the Shore we were saluted with a Cannon & on our Arrival on board the Schooner were again saluted, from hence on board a Merchant Sloop who saluted us & our having them we were again saluted from the Fort, the Capt. was polite enough to accompany us to Niagara, which we reach'd abt. 11 O Clock at Night, there are in Lake Erie two Kings Ships & three Merchantmen, they have all very convenient & pretty Accomodations for Passengers & the Provisions to supply the Different Garrisons on the Lakes & the Peltry Trade, together with the Wet & Dry Goods which are sent to Detroit & Mishalymackinet [Michilimackinac] keep them in constant Employ, they go thro Lake Erie to Detroit & to & beyond Lake Huron [*400 Batteaus this Spring*], there are in Lake Ontario but 2 Topsail Vessels, these go as Occasions require from Niagara to Oswego & Otswegotchy, & are pretty constantly employ'd tho so many Batteaus ply up & down this Lake that the far greater Part of Goods & carried in them — Lake Ontario is very deep & no Anchoring Ground near the Middle which give Lake Erie a very great Advantage —

19th.

This Morning (having gone to bed late last Night) we slept pretty sound till we were waited for at Breakfast after which went to see the Indians & purchas'd some of ther Toys,[59] as we set off for the Fort, but one of the horses we had borrow'd having run off we were supplied by Stedman with one of his — took Leave thankful for their kindness, we set off, & tho the Road we had travell'd before, it had too many Beauties to miss of entertaining us — we got to the Fort abt. 2 O Clock & immediately after

---

[59]Toys, here, trifles or curiosities.

receivd a Card from the Col. to dine with him & soon after one from Lt. Phister the Engineer to dine with him tomorrow, both wh. we accepted — the Col: ~~then~~ ^abt. 4 O Clock^ waited on us to conduct us to Dinner where were all the Officers of the Fort to whom he introduc'd us, we had a great Number of Dishes & we made a hearty Dinner to which he most politely made us welcom retir'd at 7 & receiving a polite Invitation to drink a Dish of Tea with Parson Montgomery[60] we were conducted to a Summer house in his Garden prettily situated within the Fort on the very Edge of the Bank which overlooks the Lake, the Gentlemen of the Fort being here treated us with the greatest Complaisance — Drank some Syllabub, bid them Adieu came to our Lodging got Supper & went to bed —

20th

This Morning breakfasted at home, took a walk in the 4 noon with Parson Montgomery & at 2 O Clock waited on Lt. Phister who had provided us a genteel & elegant Dinner & introduc'd us to several Officers of the Fort, who all behav'd with greatest Complais & abt. 7 in the Evening ~~returned home &~~ went to view a batteau we had thoughts of purchas.g & return'd home —

21st.

This Morning we call'd on Lt. Phister who went with us to view the Fort,[61] which is very sufficiently stockaded round & is keep in good Repair, there are inclusive of the Officers &c 160 Soliders constantly kept here, & are all under very strict Discipline — there are 8 little Guard Houses, ^in^ which are Guards Night & Day, there are 2 large Redoubts, built of Stone the Walls of which are 5 feet thick ^in^ the lower part of each there is a Large Magazine of Ammunition &c the upper Part which overlooks the River Niagara the Lake Ontario & back of the Fort for several Miles which is all clear'd Ground, are several brass Cannon which

---

[60]Chaplain James Montgomery, 10th Regiment of Foot.
[61]Before there was a Fort Niagara, the French had established on this spot the post of Fort Conti in 1679, followed by a permanent fortification in 1726, the so-called "French Castle." The British took the fort in July 1759 after a more than two-week siege.

may be fir'd on the Enemy to great Advantage as the Men are totally secure from any Assault [*Impervious to every Attack*]— ~~altho~~ there are Several Large Cannon besides these & a great Stock of small arms altho there does not appear at first View any absolute Occasion for keeping up the Fort in such Order [*a wide (word illegible) ditch the Fort contains abt 4 Acres in the middle of which is the old french fort they now ~~secure from~~ call a Citadel the Rampart, a large Ditch an outer Stockade & the (word illegible) are all (word illegible) the Fort was besieg'd by the English (word illegible) the Comm of but he dying & Sir Wm Joh(nson) being the next in Comm has all the honr of the battle*—], yet when we consider that the Indians are ever watchful [*(no danger of their going to war)*] on the Motions of the English, & look so much at their Preparations it must be prudent for them to make such a Shew as will keep these Indians in constant Awe, indeed so good an Effect has the Order & Oeconomy of this Garrison had that the wisest & greatest Chiefs of the several Indian Nations who have seen it, have from motives of sound Policy told their Bretheren as well in private & in public Speeches always to keep Friends wth whatever People were in Possession of the "great House at Niagara", whr. it is almost impossible for any Enemy (considering the Situation) to overcome, after this we went to walk ~~into~~ with Parson Mont.g who took us among other Places into their Burial Ground [*Within the horrors of this Grave / In promiscuous oer vision lie / The Bodies of two worthy men / By fatal accident did die / Death to the just is but a Gate / An Entrance into dark Rest / a Passage into heavenly Joy / Which is of all the Best*][62] which as he told was the only thing in his particular Province worth shew.g us as the Church is but very indifferent & on week Days is converted to a School — after this agreeable to the Col.'s 2nd Invitation we went to dine wt. him & to do us the greater honor he had us at his own house where he has din'd but once before since his first com.g to that Place we had here the Comp.y of the Adjutant Surgeon — Capt: of the Kings Ship & several Officers with their Ladies &c. & after Din'r was pleas'd to compliment us with a grand Band of Music we staid to drink a Dish of Coffee with his honor, & after his shew.g us every Civility we took our Departure with the strictest forms & most gracious Ceremonies — came to our Lodging & spent the Even.g there — having the Comp.y of our Fr'd Asquejoon who [word crossed out] behav'd with his usual Politeness handling a knife & fork with great grace & judgement[.]

---

[62]Fisher apparently copied this verse from one of the headstones in the cemetery he visited.

VOLUME TWO

22nd

Hav.g yesterday agreed for a ~~canoe~~ Batteau, we this Morn.g went to see
her Cork'd & benches put in for our Accomodation we went
about ransacking the whole Inhabitants for Oars paddles Sail &c. the Man
of whom we bought her not hav.g any wh. we at length with great
Difficulty found, & having our things ready to put on board we agreed
with 3 Frenchmen to take us to Montreal [*waited on Col: Smith, Comm.*
Mc.Clean & Lt. Phistene (Pfister)] & at 12 O Clock — hav.g provided an
early Dinner we embark'd, we row'd down to a Creek 12 Miles distant
which we reach'd by 6 O Clock in the evening, we had in our Course
overtook a french Battow bound for the same ^place^ our Men with hers
here went ^ashore^ we got our Supper while they smoaked & chatted &
c. ^in^ abt. half an hour we discover'd a fleet of 5 Battow who had come
from Montreal & had goods on board to take all the Way up to the
Ilionois [Indians] these were all own'd wt their Cargo's by one ^french^
Man who resided ^there^ & who had been down with loads of Furrs to
dispose of & to purchase these Goods, he staid a little time with us & his
Canoes were are conducted by Paddles, the french under stand.g that
better than row.g oars their Complexion is very coppery & they go naked
as Indians indeed some more so & it is only from their Eyes & their hair
that they can be distinguished, if their whole Bodies are uncover'd they
will be sure to have a thick corse woolen Cap on which they wear Day &
Night winter & Summer [this its probable proceeds from their long
Winters wh. consist of 5 Months dur.g which time they habituate
themselves to such a Way of living that they find the Summer too short
~~the~~ to break themselves of —][.] Their Food they are as little nice about,

except that they are not Cannibals, they are equally Lazy, & like the Indians the prefer work.g in the Night to the Day, ours however were much better than the common run, they had both Jackets & Shirts. They are fond of their Pipe to a very great Excess, & nothing persuasive or threatening or hurrying would induce them to leave it, at their periodical smoakings — we staid here till 8 O Clock [*spoke (hailed) several Boats bound from Schenectady for Niagara*], when the Men agreeable to french Custom got into the Boats & we set off, ~~all the Men in each Boat, now began to sing~~ & with a remarkable fine Evening the moon shining & on the calm Lake, the Men as happy as they are ignorant & miserable rowd ^& smoak'd^ & sung the whole Night, we seeking Sleep with a Blanket thown over us, ~~they~~

23rd

We wak'd this Morning & found our Men had row'd us abt. 20 Mile on, in we all landed & boiling some Chocolate for Breakfast, as soon as we had finish'd it & the Men theirs, they with the other Boats Crew [*with their pipes in Mouths*] all round a fine fire fell insensibly into a sound sleep which they enjoy'd with much snoaring for abt. 4 hours — when we set off & got abt. 8 Miles further to Dinner which was compos'd of some fresh Meat we brought from Niagara — in the After. the Wind coming up strong a head & it beginning ^to rain^ we contented ^ourselves^ [*for abt an ho.*] with the thoughts of staying here all Night, & after eating a hearty supper of Pidgeons & Kildeas [killdeers] we laid ourselves down in our tent & made full Compensation for the Loss of Sleep the Night before by tak.g one long Nap the whole Night tho the rain did not cease to Beat on us thro the tent —

24.

I rose early this Morn.g & finding a fair Wind I calld up my Companions & the Boatmen with the agreeable Intelligence [*the other french Boat fearg to come out —*] & ~~had~~ ^we^ got on abt. 8 Mile when the Wind blow.g rather too hard we thought best to put in, which we did for abt. an hour, here we met 2 Boats bound for Detroit, on Consultation we agreed to push forw'd & sail'd with a fine fair Wind till abt. 10 O Clock when the Swell increas'd much in the Lake, we would now very willingly put into some Port but the Surf being high on the Shore made us very cautious, till abt. 11 O Clock when the wind still continuing to increase, & we judging ~~it al~~ every moment we staid out an absolute Risque of our Lives, we thought best to run the Chance of breaking our boat to Pieces on the Beach than hazard our lives any longer in such a tempest we accordingly run her directly towards the Shore, & she most fortunately for herself & all our Goods & Chattles together with our Provis. & Kitchen & Furniture, escapd the Rocks & got on a soft sandy Beach, while we with all possible Speed, our Fright addg to our Strength immediately unloaded her ~~& the beach~~ halld ^her^ upon the Beach, which now cut a curious Figure, being confusedly decorated with our kittle ^our Furniture consisting^ frying Pan, mugs Cups dishes Plates, Knives, our Bags of Bread, our Case & Cags of Liquor, Trunks of Cloaths tent [*oars Poles & Paddles*] &c.&c. — here we staid till 5 O Clock in the Evening when the wind lulling & we pretty much compos'd got on board & proceeded as far as Braddocks Bay [*40 Mile*], where we enchamp'd, when it soon after began ^to rain^ which notwithstandg we slept very sound —

25th

Rose this Morning, got our Breakfast.& sat of with a gentle Breeze but quite fair on till One O Clock, when it blowing too hard we put in, unloaded our Boat & got ~~our~~ Dinner [*a duck*] after which the wind lulling we got on board, & saild along till 7 O Clock, when we went on Shore & enchamp'd — 50 Mile this Day —

40

26th

Rose early [*Cold Mornings*] & being very desirous to proceed, we breakfd on board, & got within 8 Mile of Oswego to Dinner. & sat off abt. 3 & at 5 reachd Oswego [*not havg had our Cloaths off ever since we left Niagara we went to bathe in the River got a Clean Shirt &c wh.*] as the Sight of a few whites was pleasing we went up to the Fort, got some Potatoes, Sallad & Milk, & on our return found some Indians who had been on the Lake fishing & had caught a fine parcel of Salmon, amongst these was the King of the Caiujahs [Cayugas] & some Onondago's,[63] they wanted us to barter some Bread for some Fish, on wch. we gave them 1 Doz Buiscuit, they then presented us With 2 large fresh Salmon & some Eels — on one of these Salmon we made a general Feast including our Men — & after this enchamp'd — here for the first Night since we left Niagara we were much troubled with Muskitos

27th.

Rose at 4 this Morning, & found some Indians who had come to pay us a friendly Visit before we departed, tho they were not a little drunk, they made us understand by means of an empty Bottle, that they wanted some Rum, in our Defence as there were to the number of 30 there we gave them some, bid them adieu & took our Departure, we found a very high Swell in the Lake which prognosticates a high Wind, we breakfas.d on board & th got abt. 20 Mile on when we put ashore in a good Harbour & din'd on the Salmon we had left & had not been here long before a high wind came on, wh. prevented us from leaving it till 7 O Clock — this Afternoon our Men proposing to row all Night took a Nap of a few hours. here we bath'd & oct [?] off — a fine moon Evening, we sat up till 10 O Clock when each wrapp.g himself up in a Blanket fell back on some Bearskins & did not wake till

June [July] 28.

when waking abt. Sunrise we found ourselves abt. 20 Miles further on our Journey, with an Indian Canoe with 2 Men 1 Squaw & some Children on they were bound for Oswego with some Deer Skins to sell & just call'd on us for a little Rum which we gave them, the men hav.g slept abt. 2 hours we went on & got to the mouth of L'Assomption Riviere[64] to breakfast after wh. we rowed on to Traverse Point[65] when the wind rising,

[63]On the Cayugas, see Marian E. White, William E. Engelbrecht, and Elisabeth Tooker, "Cayuga." In *Handbook of North American Indians.* Vol. 15, *Northeast,* ed. Bruce G. Trigger (Washington, DC: Smithsonian Institution, 1978), 500–04.

[64]L'Assumption River, here present-day South Branch Sandy Creek, town of Ellisburg, Jefferson County.

[65]Stony Point, town of Henderson, Jefferson County.

we were oblig'd to stay here. abt. 2 hours went a Gunning & the wind falling we sat off for One of the Gallot Isles[66] which we reach'd — here we din'd, on some Snipes we had kill'd, & the Wind continuing rather too high to venture so far out as we should be oblig'd to do [*Dangerous to venture far out on acct. Gales of Wind*] the first land we are to reach being 12 [number crossed out] Miles dist. so we concluded to wait till Evening in hopes the Wind wd. fall with the Sun — our men all went asleep while we diverted ourselves with building a Peer with Stones which being very handy & we industrious soon made to cut by no means a contemptible figure, as it will serve for future Travellers ^for a Port^, in case of meet.g a Gale of Wind near an Island which is entirely surrounded with Crags — abt. 7 agreeable to Expectation it fall.g calm we embark'd & our men being very spirited we got to C[blank] Island a little after 10 [*4 Little Islands all in view with the main land at a Distance*] — our men went ashore & as it was too stony to pitch a tent we concluded to lay on board —

June [July] 29th

We rose abt. Day light & our men mistaking the Place we lay in thinking it the mouth of [blank] Bay, they took a wrong course and landed us on L'Enfan Pirdu Island[67] near 10 mile out of the Way — here we went a gunning got some Snipe & Pidgeons & sat off breakfasted on board, & abt. 11 O Clock we reach'd the mouth of the St. Lawrence [*Missisauger Fort*][68] when a fine Breeze springing up we hoisted our Sail & came along by the Sides of several Islands, — while we [word crossed out] left behind us a strait & pretty Avenue which afforded a very pleasing Prospect [*many pretty Islands in view*] — after a few miles the River narrows to abt. 2 or 3 Mile wide — & a few miles further on we approach the Milles Isles[69] [*or 1000 Islands, very properly so calld* narrow ^*width 3 to 5 Mile*^ *as soon as we get among them* —] the Idea of a great number of Islands of Sizes so various & irregular must naturally lead one

---

[66] Isle aux Gallots, today's Galloo Island, town of Henderson, Jefferson County.

[67] The small Isle L'Enfant Perdu, which no longer exists, was located in the St. Lawrence River southwest of present-day Wolf Island.

[68] Missassaugas, the Native people. Probably a reference to Fort Frontenac at Cadaraqui, later Kingston, Ont.

[69] The Thousand Islands.

to expect a Sight which would be as new as entertain.g & agreeable —
the Sight of them by no means disappointed me nothing could be finer,
Large & small [letters crossed out] Islands of every Size from 10 feet to
miles in length some of them partly overflow'd others but a little Way, &
others high out of the Water, some sandy some rocky, some verdant to
the Waters Edge, while trees of & [word illegible] Shrubs of every
Tribe & hew [*particular the Pine Cedar Aspen & Hemlock —*] adornd their
Borders, abt. 6 O Clock the winds dying away the Sight of a beautiful one
invited to take Shelter there that Evening we came to the Delightfulness
of the many beautiful objects around, the great variety of the Islands the
smooth Surface of the Water — & to heighten the Scene a serene calm &
clear Sky, not a Cloud to be seen, save a few in the West, which serv'd
only to beautify & embellish & ~~heighten~~ ^perfect^ the ~~Scene View~~. Whole
never did I see a finer Evening all this [page tear] [words illegible]
combin'd to make picturesque grand, & Sturgeons are now jumping &
clashing on the Silver Lake & Ducks & Loons & Geese with their varied
Notes make the fary Landres — We took a Dive into the Water a
convenient place offer.g at the End of our Island — the Water was so
excessive clear that we could see the Bottom at a gre.t Depht — By this
time we recd a Visit from 2 of the Messisaugaw [Missassaugas] Indians,
who seeing a large Tree on fire (wh. we did to disperse the Muskitos)
judg'd Some whites were there & concluded to come & see us — after
smoakg a Pipe & enjoying the Moonlight Eve — they took leave of us —
Slept on board [page tear]

June [July] 30th.

Rose abt. Sunrise came along thro a Continuation of the Milles Isles,
which if possible were more beautiful than what we saw the Evening
before — ^water clear^ We breakfasted on the Point of an Island of abt.
1/2 an Acre, in the midst of a multitude of other very little ones to the
number of 26 all in Sight, the beautiful Irregulatity of these surpass'd any
thing of the kind I have seen — The Situation we were on being a little
elevated gave us an Qpportunity of viewing the whole to a very great
Advantage, & the Islands being so small that our Eyes were able to
extend to the whole of them at once — we saw an Indian ^Canoe^ at a
great Distance, who notwithstanding we row'd very fast. they soon came
up with us, when we foun.d only a Wom.n & 2 little Children & were

not a little surpris'd to find that they should get up wth us when we had
4 Men row.g — we gave them Buiscuit & Bullets & in our turn receiv'd
of them some p.s of smoak'd Venison & Eels which were exceeding good
[*Eels, Venison — paddles 30 In view Beautiful Rivers Nature artless &
unadorn'd*] — in going down the River I killd 2 Loons they are a fine
large Beautiful Bird, their head a very glossy Plumage, the upper part of
their Necks very regularly strip'd the lower part a shin'g Blue, their
Breast & Belly is as white as Snow, their Wings & back regularly spotted
with white, the ground being a shining dark brown — of this Bird there
are a great many, as also the Bald & black Eagle, Pidgeons Duck, &
almost every other kind of Bird both in the Lake & all the Rivers we have
pass'd thro' — also a great Number of Deer, Bears, Wolves, Otters,
Fishers, Beavers, Martins, Foxes, Panthers &c. — we din'd on a little
Island of Rocks near the Termination of the Milles Isles — on a Fowl &
some Fish & Potatoes, & a fine Breeze of wind springing up we hurried
away, & leaving the milles Isles we came down the beautiful River abt. 2
Mile wide, it narrow.g as soon as we leave them. & a gentle Cur.t assist.g
our sail.g we came down with great Speed, meet.g many Indian Canoes,
but as the wind blew so fresh, they did not attempt to board us — We
reach'd Oswegotchy abt. 6 O Clock, the nobleness of the River for last 12
Mile was uncommonly fine & Weadth its Straitness, & the regularity of
its borders is uncommonly fine, we have a view all the Way from
Oswegotchy to the Milles Isles, during all which Space there is not a ~~hill~~
hill a Point or Bay to deprive it of uniformity & order — Oswegotchy is a
french built Fort[70] situated ~~in~~ at the head of a Bay abt. 1/2 Mile from, the
River [*33 Soldiers, 27 f Cannon*] the greater part of the Goods carried
from Montreal & Qu[ebec]. are landed here, & are carried across the
Lake in the Vessels to Niagara — this Fort is in a decaying Situation, the
Stockages being almost all moulder'd away, hav.g a Letter from Genl.
Gage[71] & one from Col. Smith to Petrifu the — Commanding Officer who
invited us to supper, & to lodge with him so long as we staid, wh. we
accepted, we sat down to a very genteel Supper & a house to lodge in
being so great a Novelty, not having seen one except at Oswego~~tachy~~
since we left Niagara we slept very comfortably —

---

[70]Fort Oswegatchie, at the mouth of the Oswegatchie River at present-day Ogdensburg, NY, had
been established by the French in 1749 as Fort de La Présentation.

[71]General Thomas Gage (1719–87), at the time commander in chief of North American British forces.

July 31st.

This morning we took a walk with the Capt: into a large Garden
containing several Acres which he has in very pretty Order the Soil is
altogether one continued heap of rich black mould & yielded every thing
with the greatest Luxuriance when we came back, we heard of a French
Boat being come down, from whom we might get a Pilot, to take us thro
the Rapids, this the Capt. was sorry to hear as it depriv'd him of our Co.
it being uncertain when another might come [*we agreed with him*], we
went to Breakfast & the Capt; ordering his Bat. to be ready we sent our
Bat. down to Fort William Augt.[72] & follow'd in the Capt.s. — This Fort
is 9 Mile from Oswegothy & advantageous situated on an Island [*B. Vue
perdu*][73] — This little Place [*with only 400 men*] formidably resisted when
in the hands of the French Gl. Amherst[74] wth. an Army of 14,000 Men, it
be.g almost inaccessible, till at the End of 15 Days, the french losing
almost all their Men & the Fort itself almost levelld with the Ground it
was ceded & Now lays in a ruinous State with only 2 Soldiers to keep it
in Possession, it was built very strong and judiciously by an ingenious
Engineer am.g the French who had some excellent Engineers among them
last War — we walk'd all round it on a Platform under wh. the Soldiers
Barracks ~~are~~, ^were^ there is no house now standing but the Remains of
an old french theatre — we staid here abt. an hour & the Capt:
Presenting us wth. some fish we bid adieu [*all the Chimnies(,) Din'd on
board*] — soon leaving this Place we come into a swift rapd. wh. is not of
long Continuance as likewise 2 or 3 others, when we go very swift but
not till we come to Long Saut Rapid[75] have we much Reason to fear, we
went so fast for abt. 2 or 3 Mile that we could not count the Trees as we
pass'd them, after this there is a current where our Men stopd to smoak
their Pipes some time till we were down to the swiftest Rapid in the
whole River, tho very deep there was a high Sea which roar'd & foam'd
frightfully, by going very near the Shore we run where the Waves were
not very high tho our flight was so swift that we could not perceive any
thing we pass'd, the whole seem'd one mixd confusd angry Element, we

---

[72]Fort William Augustus on present-day Chimney Island in the St. Lawrence, about four miles
downriver from Ogdensburg. It was built to replace Fort Levis, which had been bombarded and destroyed
by General Amherst in 1760.

[73]"B. *Vue perdu*," perhaps intending *veux perdu*, literally "wish lost."

[74]General Jeffrey Amherst (1717–97), from 1760–63 the military governor of Canada. At the time
of Fisher's travels, he held the rank of Lieutenant-General of the Ordnance.

[75]Long Sault, a rapid in the St. Lawrence River east of present-day Cornwall, Ont.

got out of this & found we had run 9 Mile in 3/4 of an hour, this has been done our men assurd us in 1/4 — but they stopp.g made us so much longer than usual — but this Act. I am induc'd to doubt, tho I believe a considerable part of the Distance we came at that Rate [*the whole Day one continued beautiful Scene*] — we reach'd a little Indian Village abt. 60 Mile below Fort Wm.[76] & meeting with ~~some~~ ^a^ genteel Frenchman who resided there he ask'd to his house & cook'd our Fish on which we suppd very heartily — he gave us a Room where we put our Mattrasses & lodg'd very comfortably —

~~July 2d~~ Aug.t 1st.

Rose early this Morning & took a walk round the Village, there are 31 houses here of the Indians, who are of the Iroquois^ or Mohawk^ Nation, & 400 Indians, besides 2 Chu & 2 french houses — the greater Part of these houses are ^built^ by Stakes being drove into the Ground & bark along the Inside, the Cracks & Vac.^t^ are filled with a Cement made of Clay — & the others are built of Logs which are very tolerably squa'd the Indians are more civilis'd than any ~~nation~~ ^other^ we have seen except the ~~The~~^ir Brethren^ Mohawks, at 9 O Clock we went to the Chappel where the Priest gave us a French Sermon, very sensible tho his Appearance ~~nor~~ ^&^ Delivery were by ~~any~~ ^no^ means graceful After this in another part of the Chappel we went to Mass where ~~Were~~ abt. 150 Indians attended, they are all ^in^ this Village of the Roman Catholic Religion they behav'd very ^well^ I never was in a Place of Worship [word illegible] was more Riverence & Respect paid to time & Place — they sung particularly the Women whose Voices are remarkably soft admirably well, & with great Propriety after Mass we went among the Indian Houses to see for trinkets wh. we found in most of the Indian Houses are hung up in some R: C: Pictures — we bid our Landlord ^adieu^ thank'd him for his Civilities & at 12 O Clock got on board where we soon after din'd we got into the Lake St. Francois [Lake St.

---

[76]This is the Indian mission village of St. Regis or Akwesasne (Mohawk, *ahkwesáhsne*, commonly translated "where the partridge drums," although it also carries the meaning "partridge place"), established by about the mid-eighteenth century. Today the native community of Akwesasne sits astride the U.S./ Canadian border as the St. Regis Mohawk Reservation and the St. Regis Mohawk Reserve. See William A. Starna and Jack Campisi, "When Two Are One: The Mohawk Indian Community at St. Regis (Akwesasne)." *European Review of Native American Studies* 14, no. 2 (2000): 39–45.

Francis] in abt. an hour where the Current left us, soon after came on a very violent Storm with Thunder Lightening & rain wh. oblig'd us to put into an Island, where we staid till 4 O Clock — it clearing up & a fair Wind offering we sail'd a few miles when our Passage occasion'd by a number of ~~little~~ Islands was so narrow & crooked we were oblig'd to row — we came along till near 10 O Clock when we went ashore to the house of a ^French^ Man who pilots all Boats coming down except the Indians for which he receives 4 Dollars each — but if he takes several down together he receives no more — here we found Man Wife, & 7 Children with others who did not live there with Dog Cat &c, ^all in gt Confusion^ so that when we got there with all our men in number 9 wh fill'd their house pretty well, as they had but one Room, & that very little, & as it had rain'd the ground wet as well as our Tent & Sail we ask'd for floor Room to put our Mattrasses on, which notwithstanding a Difficulty to clear much Ground they granted us with all french Politeness [*we supp'd on ^our^ Chocolate wh. we got leave to cook, & had a comfortable Chest for our Table — & as we were entire Strangers handed us a Chair which was all their home afforded —*] — as french are very fond of conversation, & the Gentleman of the house an old Acquaintance of our Battow Men, tho. sat up till 2 O Clock in the morning (with the Children of the house from 4 years old & upwards with pipes in the Mouths) smoking & talk.g so that I got little Sleep that Night —

August 2d.

Rose early this Morning, came down abt. 24 Mile hav.g several very dangerous Rapids the Water in many Places being shallow & sometimes the Crags peeping out of the Water, they were not however near so swift as we pass'd thro before [*the last 24 Mile*] we came down, as well as 4 Miles & we pass'd the Night before is a beautiful verdant Bank, at first ~~rising~~ but abt. 20 feet from the Surface of the water but gradually rising as we go down the River, ^beyond^ which the Land is rich & level, & ~~houses~~ ^settlements^ all that Distance on the West Side of the River equidistant from each other, the whole Land on the Water being divided into 3 Acre Lots [*little log houses*] & settled by Persons who liv'd in Montreal, & many of ~~them~~ ^whom were^ once in good Circumstances ^are^ now doomd to undergo ~~the~~ a Life of Labour & Toil, at this they do not [word illegible] as other Nations do, they enjoy the present &

without thinking of the past, it is a maxim among them that they cease to be frenchman when they cease to be gay — notwithstanding this they are apt to be much sunk down at ~~the Loss of~~ ^meeting^ any misfortune, ~~but~~ ^&^ their Trouble is much ~~&~~ ^but^ short, they soon forget ~~it~~, & drown them in Talk — we stopd at a Mile [*where our men breakfasted*], & sent up to a little Village for some fresh Bread & Milk, which being a Rarity we made a hearty breakfast of, ascending the Bank which gave a pretty Exhibition of every thing round us, several Islands which puzzled us to know the ^true^ Course of the River, & several pretty Caskades in Sight, While we were here several Rafts [*of boards*] passed by on their Way to Montreal seeing them go down the Rapids very curious — after this we sat off & musterd our Resolution, for passing some Rapids, which were much more Dangerous & steep than any we had come to — these are call'd the Cedres & les Cascades or le Trout[77] — we came to them & all but the last we escap'd without much Danger, in descending these being very steep we shipd a large Sea which came fore & Aft on the Side I sat & wet me all over our Fear here was increas'd by our hav.g just before hit on a Rock tho very slightly our going so swift gave us a considerable Shock — in this Place 180 People were lost of the Army in com.g down to take Montreal [*General Amherst*] not hav.g Pilots on board — tho since that few accidents have happen'd — here we stop'd our Pilot left us we bal'd our Boat & sat off — the Parrot Island[78] appear'd at a Distance & that & the ^high^ Land opposite being ~~highly~~ ^richly^ cultivated, the Banks gently sloping to the Water Edge & clothd with every kind ^of Grain^ which being now ripening appeard to great Advantage — ~~tho~~ we now come into a very thick settled Country the Shores on either side being one continued Street, we came ~~to~~ at Cachenouaga [Caughnawaga], a large Indian Town[79] went a little Way into, but fearing we could not see the whole & get to Montreal that Night we concluded to come here a few Days hence, we went on board & din'd, this Day we killd the last of 6 Chickens we had bought at Fort Stannix & carried up to Niagara — a Woman her Daughter & Son requesting us to take them in our Boat ~~so~~

---

[77]"The cedres [cèdres]" refers to "cedars"; "les cascades" means "the waterfalls." The reference here is generally to the series of rapids that begins upriver from Montreal and then, becoming the Lachine Rapids, runs between the Island of Montreal and the south bank of the St. Lawrence River. The meaning behind Fisher's "le trout" is unknown.

[78]Ile Perrot, an island just west of the Island of Montreal.

[79]The native community of Caughnawaga (Mohawk *kahnawà·ke* 'at the rapids'), established by the late seventeenth century, is today the Kahnawake (Caughnawaga) Reserve. See Fenton and Tooker, "Mohawk."

Montreal 1774

far a few miles we took them in & landed them at the Place, we now come into the last Rapid we are to see which is in sight of Monreal & is rather Dangerous, we got over it with only one thump & reachd Monreal abt. 4 O Clock the Town look'd very pretty coming to it as we came right on it all at once in front where it appeard to the greatest Advantage — we were met on the Landing Place by a great Number of Gentlemen, but we being very dirty, made the best of the our Way thro' them, & took up our Lodgings at [blank] [word crossed out] we staid in the house this Evening got an early Supper & went to bed —

August 3d

After Breakfast this Morning we waited on Wm. Dobie a Gent, to whom we had a Letter of Introduction & to ——— Grant who lives in the same house [*at his house we met with Davidson a Gentleman from England who*

now lives in Canada —][80] the former gave us a polite Invit.a to Dinner
tomorrow which we accepted the latter was going off to Quebeck &
appologiz'd for his not being able to wait on us — we afterwards went to
Lawrence Ert[blank] a french Gentleman, who invited us to to dine with
him the Day after tomorrow which we accepted we came to our Lodgings
soon after were waited on [_we met with_] by Wm. Dobie & L. Ermatinger[81]
who call'd on us to view some of the Curiosities of the Place — we first
went to the Seminary,[82] thro the hall into the Garden which contains abt.
3 Acres, is very regularly laid out with a great variety of flowrs shrubs,
Fruit Trees & &c. the walks in it are wide & smooth & regular, the Plan
is very pretty & directly in the french Taste, there are several romantic
Retreats, large Summer Houses &c. where Gentleman may always freely
resort as if it were their own — ~~th~~ we go from the ~~thro~~ ^up^ a Large
high Stone Stair Case into the hall wh. is very spacious ornament.d with
Images & Pictures & thro several large Rooms to the Church which is
very grand & elegant the Roof is arch'd, & the whole has an awful &
solemn Appearance the Altar is large & very curiously decorated — this
Building is in front abt. 400 feet — it is own'd by the Seminaries
[_Seminaries dress in a black Robe girded abt them — a bag always hanging_
with a Book in it V. their Riches where arises] who educate Children only
who are to officiate as Romish Priests — we next went to the Fryars, at
the Door there are two Images, the Patrons of their Order — one of the
Fryars very politely receivd us, took us thro the various Appartments, wh.
except a few large Rooms is divided into a great Number of little
Appartments [_their Domesticity_], adjoining this is their Church which is
very large & commodious the Altar is grand — in this Place the
Protestants hold their Church [_not having one of their own sp. (their)_
English (is) bad] ^for^ which they pay a pretty considerable Rent [_6_
Fryers — posess the whole] [_Their Income—_] [_Probability of the English_
getting it —] the Fryars dress in a long ^black^ Robe, ~~but~~ with a Girdle

---

[80]Probably intending Richard Dobie (c. 1731–1805), fur trader, businessman, and militia officer,
and William Grant (1743–1810), a fur trader and Montreal merchant; _Dictionary of Canadian Biography_
5:258–61, 376–77; accessed at <http://www.biographi.ca/en/index.php>. Grant was a business acquaintance of Dobie, Lawrence Ermatinger (see note below), and Edward Chinn (see note below). Fisher
appears to have confused the first names of Dobie and Grant.

[81]Lawrence Ermatinger (1736–89), born in Switzerland, a fur trader and merchant out of Montreal
who also sold slaves. A one-time acquaintance of Richard Dobie; _Dictionary of Canadian Biography_
5:258–61. One of Lawrence's sisters-in-law married Edward Chinn. See W. Brian Stewart, _The Ermatingers_
A Nineteenth-Century Ojibwa-Canadian Family (Vancouver: University of British Columbia Press, 2007).

[82]This is Montreal's Saint Sulpice Seminary (Le Vieux Séminaire de Saint-Sulpice), the construction
of which had begun in 1684.

about them, they have a Rope with Knots ty'd in it for their Beads —
their Presence is particularly offensive, as the Dress they put on they
never pull off till it is so Rotten that it will no longer hold together — we
went into their garden which is very large, & in pretty Order — fruits,
trees. Herbs & Flowers of almost every kind — we next ~~came home &~~
went to see their Court house, the Room the Court is held in which was
then sitting is small & diminutive — the Lawyers for the most part plead
in English, but in some Cases they are under the Necessity of speaking in
French — the french are much pleasd with Juries — we came home to
Dinner, & had agree'd with Mons. Ermantinger to take a Ride but it
coming on to Rain disappointed us — [*a clearing up*] in the Evening we
took a Walk round which is 4 — Miles — the whole is wall'd in a
Rampart between a high Bank which is rais'd & the Wall which is 20 feet
high & 4 feet thick — the Situation is very much against it ^as^ a Place
of Defence a high Mountain, abt. 1 Mile from it, which directly overlooks
it, ~~this~~ here General Amherst w. his Army of 14000 Men pitchd there &
the Situation being so advantageous & his Army so formidable — the
french without Opposition, ceded the town after a very few Days[83] but
tho this Place is by no means sufficiently fortified for an Enemy so
powerful as the English it was excellently devised ~~for~~ to def.d any Attack
from the Savages & for this Purpose it was built — we spent the Evening
at the Coffee house, which ~~is~~ ^a^ very ~~genteel~~ respectable ~~of~~ Number of
Gentlemen resort to in the Evening — but inst.d of doing Business — the
house rings with the Dice — we returnd home in the Evening —

Augt. 4th

Rose early this Morning & agreeable [word illegible] Appointment hav.g
provided 2 calashes we call'd on J Davidson & took a Ride along a fine
high Bank with overlooks the River & a great Quantity of low flat
improv'd Land the houses on both Sides of the River are very near each
other & highten the View — several Island floating in the River, & the
Cascades near the Town make a beautiful Appear. we got to La Crane [La
Chine] a little Village abt. 7 O Clock, & crossed the River St. Lawrence to

---

[83]The reference is to the overwhelming forces, commanded by General Jeffrey Amherst, that had
encamped around Montreal on Sept. 7, 1760, followed the next day by the surrender of the city—and
Canada—by its governor, the marquis de Vaudreuil.

Cacheawago [Caughnawaga] a Large Indian Village near 80 Cabbins &
houses — some of wh. are of Stone which are to be seen no where else
— the Number of Indians are computed 700 — they are of the Iroquois
or Mohawk Nation, & these and those ^of the^ Village of St. Regis
describd before have deserted the Mohawk in the Time of the War &
joind the French & embrac'd their Religion — there is a here a large
Church to accomdate them the Priest I met with at his Door I receivd an
Invitation to go into his Garden & fell in ~~with~~ ^to^ a Latin Conference
on Religion &c. he is a sensible Man — we went into many of the houses
to see the manner [abbreviated word illegible] these live most ^equal^ in
the English ~~except~~ as those at St. Regis hav.g [word illegible] there is a
Stone Inclosure for the Dead with Piles of Indian Signification rais'd to
their Memory ~~of their Dead~~ — here is likewise the Remains of an old
Fort the Walls only standing[84] — we crossed the River and got to
Montreal abt. 2 O Clock, went to R. Dobies who shew'd us his Vaults of
Skins [Reason of Vault (page tear)] [*See the next Leaf which ~~the same day~~
continues the Acct began here of the Hotel Dieu (initialed) J F.*] & went to
his house to Dinner This Gentleman is of the Note as a Merchant he
ships £30,000 per Annum in Furrs to England he shew'd us the greatest
Civilities at abt. 6 O Clock we took a Walk to the Mountain of [blank]
which with the greatest Difficulty & not without considerable Doing we
ascended, & ^by^ the time we got up it was so dark that we were
depriv'd of enjoying the Motives of our going — we returned home in the
Dark not a little fatigued —

August 5.

After Breakfast we calld on Mons. Ermatinger who went with us to see
the Hotel d'Dieu[85] — on our Entrance we got into the Mans Hospital a
long Room, with beds of each Side a Fire Place between & every Bed has
~~an~~ Curtains to it, the whole is very neat clean & convenient, above this is
the Womans which is the same as below — there are ^a^ number of little
Appartments for the Nuns — after this we were shewn the Dining Room

---

[84]Fisher is viewing the remains of Fort St-Louis, erected at Caughnawaga by the French in 1725.
Its wooden palisade was replaced by stone walls in the late 1740s. The fort has been designated a National
Historic Site of Canada.

[85]Hôtel-Dieu de Montréal, one of the first hospitals to be founded in North America, is no longer
at its original location.

wher one ~~of~~ ^or^ two of the Nuns [*Ursulines*] were, they desird us to sit down — & in a few Minutes were visited by a Retinue of the Liverie'd Dames, at the head of Whom Lady Abbess appear'd, a hearty, jolly, fat old Woman, with the greatest Ceremony they sat down with us a few minutes, talkd over their happy hours & their Contentment which by the by they enjoy little of — & took us up stairs to the Drugs Room where they had a vast Quantity of every Article in that Branch — in the neatness Order, the whole is containd in large Mahogny Cases, with Glass Doors — every thing here is clean here we enterd into free Converse with the Madamoiselles, who are free conversible, without the least Reserve, their Countenances are chearful & sprightly, they have a great Appearance of good health which was probably increas'd at the Sight of the Visitors — we went into the Church which is very gay — the Nuns have an Apartment in the right Side of the Altar, & a Littice Division, with a Curtain drop'd hide them from public View — their Dress is black except a white handf. which partly appears under their Chin, & a white Cloth which comes from under their Veils hides the Forehead, & come quite down

Un Chanson chantè par [A song sung by]—

[See Appendix 1]

Journal resume'd, Vol. 3 of the same date Augt. 5 [initialed] J. F

[See Appendix 2]

VOLUME THREE

Canada &c
JMF   Vol III
1773

Montreal to Quebeck _____ _____ L 200[86]	
Montmerenci[87] _____ _____	9
Shodeir [Chaudière][88] _____ _____	8
Lorette[89] _____ _____	10
St. Johns[90] _____ _____	210
Crown Point _____ _____	120
Tecondarago [Ticonderoga] ___ ___	16
[Words illegible] _____ _____	3
Lake George _____ _____	86
Albany _____ _____	70

Aug.t 5.

They have the key of their Appartment, a pair of Scissars & their Beeds
hanging from their Girdle — we bid them Adieu & went to see the
Jesuits Church which joins the Goal [jail] he has a large & spacious
house & the Church is elegant — adjoining wh. is a Garden which
abounds with Plenty of Fruits & Vegetables — We next went to the
Congregation of the Sisters who educate the Girls of the Town as well
Protestants, as Romans, they have a pretty Church, but a late Fire has
consum'd the whole inside & nothing but the Altar is yet repair'd — We
next went to the Congregation of the Grey Sisters, where alas! are nought
but the Remains of Papal Folly. The Women here are but few & those are
old & ugly, & have now before the sad & mortifying Prospect of
becoming extinct, not a single young one to replace the Grey hairs of

---

[86] Fisher's "L" is likely an abbreviation for *lieue*, the French for "league," although it is possible that he was referring to the English "league." In either case, and unlike his estimates in miles between places provided earlier in the journal, these are inaccurate.

[87] Montmorency River and falls just downriver from the city of Quebec.

[88] Chaudière River.

[89] At present-day L'Ancienne-Lorette, west of Quebec City. A century earlier it had been the location of a Huron Indian mission.

[90] Today Saint-Jean-Sur-Richelieu, Quebec, at the foot of Lake Champlain.

those now descending to the Grave a Reason may perhaps be given their
Dress is not so becoming. They wear a brown loose camblet Gown wh.
hides ^an^ abundance of their Graces & indeed they need be self denying
to chuse this — & what perhaps tends more to mortify them, they are at
Liberty to go abroad & provide the necessaries of the house which two of
them take in Rotation. This lets them see the Diffl. of their Situation —
their Building is situated out of the Walls of the town — tho they have
now a very neat Church building set in the town — opposite wh. is a
large & elegant house where the last french Gover.r of Canada resided
this they are now converting into a Colledge for the Education of the
Roman Youths — a little Way from this is the old Fort built by Gen.l
Amherst after the Conquest merely for a Defence against the Savages it
has a great Number of Cannon & Ammunition, & a Garrison of 350 Men
are now station'd here — it is situated at the NE: end of the Town, on a
big hill of artificial Ground — but like all other English Forts in time of
Peace is going to Ruins — we went to Dinner with our Polite fr'd
Ermatinger, who introduc'c us to Major Carlton[91] & several other
Gentlemen — he provided us a gent'l & elegant Dinner, & at 5 O Clock
had 2 Calashes at his Door, when in Co. with __ __ Chin[92] & __ __
Davidson[93] we mounted. & after going out of the So. Gate we gradually
ascend a high Mountain — a little Way up is a Building belonging to the
Jesuits adjoining wh. is a large Garden surrounded by a Stone Wall —
after passing this a Beatiful Prospect opens to our View as we ascend the
hill which is richly clothd with Verdure & here & there a few Scatterd
trees — & the Summit is crown'd with a thick foliage, [beginning of
word crossed out] it descends very regularly by a great Distance till all at
once one arrives at a the Brink of a perpendicular Bank, abt. 100 feet
below the Lands are level & every Spot is fill'd with Vegetation, half way
between the Bank & River runs in wild meanders a sweetly purling [word
illegible] feeding the fertile Soil, the fences at right angles dissect the
Ground into small lots, along the Waters Edge houses are prettily rang'd,
a little from the Shore is a delightful Island, beyond this a Cascade or
Rapid, where the Water wears a hoary head, till stealing gently on it loses

---

[91] Guy Carleton (1724–1808), first Baron of Dorchester, who from 1768 to 1778 was governor of
the Province of Quebec, while at the same time serving as governor general of British North America.
He was formerly a military officer.

[92] Edward or John Chinn, brothers and widely recognized traders and merchants who operated
throughout the Great Lakes region and the St. Lawrence Valley.

[93] Earlier, on Aug. 4, Fisher writes of a J. Davidson.

its Wildness, runs itself clear _____. "And as ^it^ runs refines Till by Degrees the floating Mirror shines" carrying ones Eyes along the Silver bosom of the Stream a little further on we reach the ~~far~~ Southern Shore, where for a while the hand of Cultivation smiles & Villages appear, the Banks are low the ground in Culture gay, but there succed a Train of Mountains, under the tops of which ^we are^ ~~in wild Disorder~~ the Clouds floating in wild Disorder — when the Eye changes its Directions to the Prospects up & down the River Wh. are equally beautiful & as various — we pass on till we reach the Summit ~~of the Summit~~ of the Mount, when going thro a few Corn fields we arriv'd at a genteel house, the good Family whereof conducted us into the Garden, which is the largest & most in Order of any in Canada — two large main Walks crossing at right Angles run thro the whole & are shaded by trees the Tops of wh. meet & form an umbrageous Walk [*Delightful haunt fa for Contemplation*] the four Squares wh. these Divisions make are neatly laid our & surpass any thing I have seen for Size & Order — which are by no means the greatest Beauties of the Situations — the Prospect is immense it descends from every Side, we see the River which ~~runs on~~ ^waters^ the Wes: Side of the Island, ~~&th~~ we see the Water at the End of the Island, & all the Way along till it arrives at the town, ~~of~~ a Prospect of wch. is intercepted by a little Wood, & ~~but~~ for this we see all round the horizon mountains oerlapping each other & mingling with the Clouds far as our furthest Eye can ken — The Mons.r of the house not being at home Madam & Madamoiselle after shewing us these Beauties conducted us into an elegant Parlour, plac'd before us of the choisest of Viands, a Banquet on wh. we deliciously regal'd — bid them Adieu & return'd home not a little delighted with our Retreat —

August 6t

This Morning we had appointed to take a Ride with L: Ermatinger abt. 20 Miles down the Island, but a Prospect of rain deterr'd us from execut.g our Plan dind at home & it clearing up in the Afternoon a Pa[r]ty was made up for taking a Ride when Calashes were prepar'd for us ~~&~~ but B & D being out of the Way I went along without them, we rode out abt. 3 Mile along the Banks of the Island wh. overlook the River, to a Place call'd the Montreal Coffee house[94] where had some Bread Beef & Porter,

---

[94]A well-known tavern run by Thomas John Sullivan, an Irish immigrant. See Frank Mackey, *Black Then: Blacks and Montreal, 1780s–1880s* (Kingston: McGill-Queen's University Press, 2004), 27.

took a Walk into the Garden, back of wh. is a pretty chinese Pleasure house gayly ornamented <u>toute a la mode</u>,[95] with Spires & curved Roof — this overlooks a beautiful improv'd Country — we returnd home in the Evening, thence to Coffee house & suppd with Davidson —

August 7t.

This Morning we had appointed for our Departure but from the Persuasions of some Gentlemen & a Party form'd for a little Excursion we concluded to stay 2 Days longer in a Place we had spent ^our time^ so agreeably — abt. 9 O Clock in Co. wt. Davidson & Chin we sat out & rode thro a fine rich Country but very bad rode to the [blank] a little Village situated on the west Side of the Is.d we took a Walk to see a curious Mill wh. goes only by the Rapidity of the Water in its natural Course. the Wheels There are 3 Water Wheels all turn'd by this Means the Building is large but it manufactures only for the Consumption of the Inhabitants of the Island — from this Place we have a pretty view of the Isle of Jesus[96] — divided from this but by a little Water — We returnd home abt. 5 O Clock went to see our Fr'd R Dobie, who presented me with a very curious Seal Skin Coat curiously ornamented with Indian Work — we return'd home where Davidson & Chin came to see us & suppd —

August 8t

The Officers of the Fort & some Gentl.n on their Travels having last Night taken Possession of our Room & we fearing they would not go to Bed soon we put our Mattrasses below & went to Bed in a Dark Room wh. occasiond us lay on Bed till 8 O Clock this Morn.g soon after which we were waited on by L Ermatinger to shew us the Way to the Parish Church — we went along & found that large Church so full that we could scarcely pass, we however got a very near Place to the Altar — that we heard & saw every Minutiae — we had after Mass a Sermon deliver'd

---

[95] *Tout à la mode*, meaning "in the latest fashion."
[96] Ile Jésus, on the north side of the island of Montreal.

by a hearty stout Man with a loud Voice, but he spoke so very fast that we could not understand him — we left this Place & went to the Protestant where a french Clergyman officiated, he spoke English so bad that ^it^ was with great attention we heard him — his Discourse was however sensible — we went after Church to Dinner with Patterson & Kay at the house of the former these are the first Merchants in the Place, abt. 6 O Clock they took a Walk with us to the Parade, where the Soldiers exercise every Evenig — returnd home in the Eve.ng supp.g with Kay & Davidson.

[See Appendix 3]

August — 9t

Rose early this Morning got our things on board our good old Frigate, breakfast'd & abt. 7 O Clock sat off with a fine Current to speed our Course, the River exhibited some pretty scenes a Number of little Islands & &c. abt. 11 O Clock a fine fresh Gale sprung up, we hoisted our Mainsail — & din'd on Board & got abt. 80 Mile down the River by Dusk we went ashore, beg'd leave to lay our Mattrasses on the Floor ^of the house of a poor Peasant^ — granted — had our Victuals brought in, a neat Table laid — a fine roasted Piece of Beef Potatoes good Wine &c. —, beg'd the favour of Mon. Madam & Madamoiselle to sup with us, to wh. they agree'd, after Supper Madamoiselle got a Fiddle to shew us her Skill in the Art of Music, wh. we on our appearing pleas'd she dispatch'd an Express to summon some of the Neighbours to the house, who were not delinquent in attending, soon the house was throng the ^jovial^ Dance began the bare leg'd Dancers trip'd the Flour with great Agility, according with the[remainder of word illegible] Nymph — who did not think amiss to stoop to mix with the Peasants of the River, who all admir.'d her, she was the prettiest french Girl I have seen since I have been in Canada, extremely polite & had a Sensibility in her Countenance which would have claim'd a Preference in most Places & was conspicuous among the others — 10 O Clock arriv'd we should have been glad to have gone to bed, our Wishes were vain, they had taken Possession of our Room — we sat up a long time with great Impatience indulging ourselves with the Novelty of the Scene at Past 12 by some hint we dropd the merry Ditty was put an End to we got Possession of our Room — &c.

August 10th.

Rose abt. 4 this Morning a fair Wind we came along with a fair Wind, wh. after a while proving too high as we were in a Lake — we run up a little Creek abt. 1/2 Mile to a french farm from whom we got some Bread & Milk after ~~Supper~~ ^Breakfast^ as we were but 30 Miles from Trois Rivieres [Trois—Rivières], we concluded to go there by Land & by the time [letters illegible] could arrive we might have seen every thing curious in the Place we accordingly mounted a very wooden Calash wh. carried us along a very pretty Creek wh. we overlooked to the next Post where we got another — we now went on very merrily changing our horse every 2 & 3 Leagues — we reach'd Trois Rivieres abt. 2 O Clock, where we din'd we went after Dinner to view the Nunnery & the manufactury of the Bark Canoes wh. are made here in great Numbers — we afterwards went to see the young; Ladies ~~of the ladies~~ of the City, who all here as well as at Montreal & Quebeck are put into a Nunnery & taught to work in the same Manner — of those secluded from the World ~~injoy~~ & they make many Articles for Sale — The Ladies here as well as in other Parts of Canada want Charms — Trois Rivieres is the 3rd District of Canada. the Capital is situated on the west mouth of a Creek which after running a little way up into the Country divides into 3 Channels from wh. this takes its Name — it is 3d. City in Canada for Size & Trade — There are abt. 200 houses in it — among wh. is the Nunnery wh. is of the Ursuline Order with Church adjoining — the Recolet's Convent wh. a Church Garden &c. — & the Jesuits. it stands on a high Bank wh. over looks the River St. Lawrence to the SE: & ~~a~~ ^3^ Rivers [Trois—Rivières] to the NEW — we left this Place abt. 5 O Clock with a fine Breeze & got abt. 12 Miles when we went ashore, got leave of a french Family to lodge there eat for Supper some Pidgeons we had brought from 3 Rivers.

August 11th.

A Fine Gale offering our Battowmen call'd us up abt. 3 O Clock this with the Tide urg'd us on very speedily, we came by some beautiful Situations on the River. had very often so fair a View up & down the River that we lost the Land except on both Sides of us — abt. 12 O Clock we came to, & under [word crossed out] ^a fine high^ Bank where we were invited by a beautiful Cascade falling from top of the hill in many pretty

Breaks we went with great Difficulty up to the Summer [summit] — ~~from~~ where however we were well paid for our Trouble, the fine Prospect we had of a vast improv'd Tract of Country on the opposite Shore wh. being thick settled & the houses white had a very happy Effect in producing a variety to beautify the Scene we walk'd a little while ^here^ & found by chance a ♭ delightful Path wh. led winding down the Hill, thro a most Romantic thicket — we din'd below on some Pidgeons & Potatoes — & abt. 2 sat off for Quebeck — we ~~saw~~ ^came by^ at a Distance the Cove in wh. Wolf[97] landed from the opposite Side & just saw a part of the Walls on the Top of a monstrous hill — we came to in the Harbour where laid abt. 18 Topsail Vessels & a great Number of smaller ones — we landed went up to the Coffee house where we spoke for our Lodgings — & were soon after hear'd of by — Wilcocks & J. Swift to whom we had Letters of Introduction who waited on us & gave us an Invitation to dine with them 2 follow.g Days. Swift staid & supped with us —

August 12t.

This Morning we proceeded to the Delivery of several of our Letters the Gentlemen behav'd with the greatest Civility — we came back to the Coffee house — then took a little walk along the lower town — they have one or two convenient Wharfs built — but most of the Vessels load in the Stream. we went a little Way up the Town along the Water Side where the High perpendicular Rocks above appear very frightful — we went to the house of our Fr'd Wilcocks where we din'd in Co. wth. Woolsey[98] — staid Coffee & took a Walk [*round the Town Suburbs &c Height of Wall—*] round the Walls of the Town which are abt. 3 Mile round, very high, & thick & appear entirely impregnable — ~~the g~~ we return'd [word crossed out] by the Way of the Govr.s Gardens[99] which commands a beautiful View of the St. Lawrence which it overlooks from a steep high inaccessible hill, we see the Island of Orleans[100] & Point Levy

---

[97]General James Wolfe (1727–59), who led the victorious British forces on the Plains of Abraham (Quebec City) in 1759.

[98]Probably John William Woolsey, a merchant and businessman in Quebec City. As a militia officer during the American siege of the city in 1775–76, he was made prisoner and taken to Philadelphia; *Dictionary of Canadian Biography* 8:952–53; accessed at <http://www.biographi.ca/en/index.php>.

[99]Governor's Garden, southwest of the Saint-Louis fort and chateau. The present-day landmark, the Fairmont Château Frontenac Hotel, is close by.

[100]Ile d'Orléans, in the St. Lawrence just downriver from Quebec City.

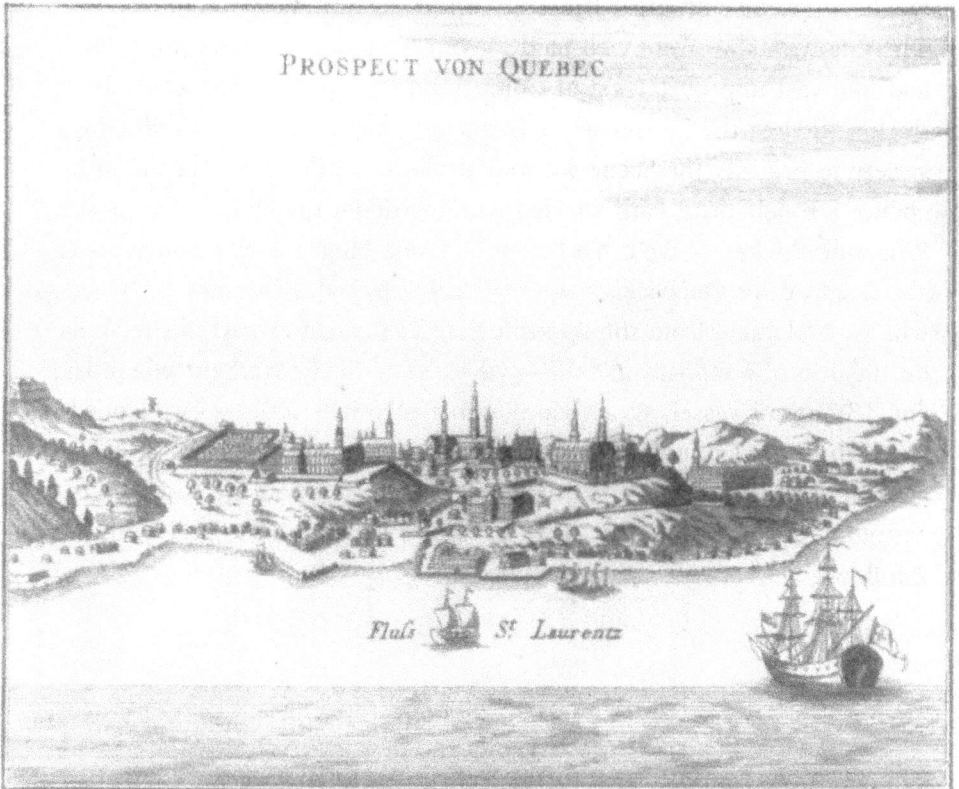

Quebec 1789

on the former of the wh. is a great tract of improv'd Country to this Place [*Governors Garden return'd home* ♭] the Gentlemen & Ladies of the Town resort every Evening & while they stroll thro the Serpentine Walks or set themselves on Chairs which are here & there they are seneraded with a fine Band of Musick — we returnd home in the Even.g

13th.

This Morning we breakfasted wt. our Fr'ds Davidson & Lees, & set out for Montmerenci [Montmorency] [*Went to Montmerenci — returnd & dind wh. Swift — took a Walk, sup'd wth. Swift —*] in Co. with Davidson Swift & Wilcocks & arriv'd after riding about 8 Miles thro' a fine improv'd Country at the celebrated Falls of Montmerenci [*Fall 90 Wide 160 High*(,) *Trout*] beautiful regular & I climb with vast Difficulty &

Danger the hill near the Falls hitherto deem'd insurmable — eat some
Bread & Cheese drank some Porter & Wine went abt 1 1/2 Mile above to
the Steps, This is the most pleasg beautiful Romantic regular Place in
Nature —

Aug. 14th

Breakf. this Morning wt. E. Harrison Esq. [*Breakf. Harrison 14th a Party
of 12 went to Shodeir (Chaudière) din'd sup'd 11 0 Clock*][101] who has
invited us on a Party to Shodur [Chaudière] we sat off from his Wharf in
Co. with abt. 12 of our Aryerant [?] & row'd along with the tide to the
opposite Side abt. 7 Mile up the River when we got out went to a little
Hut, cook'd some Beaf stake drank &c. & set off abt. 3 O Clock for the
Falls & got to them in 1/2 hour Romantic wild enchanting very wide 60
ft. high far preferable to Montmerenci returnd to hut eat some Lamb &c
for Supper & got home abt 11 O Clock at Night —

15

Breakfasted at Davidson & Lees who form'd a Large Party to go to Lorete
[Lorette] [*Breakfast 15 at Davison & Lees went with a Large Party to
Lorrette falls — Tonight — Dance — home*] a little Indian Village of abt.
60 houses we set off at 9 got there at 10 abt. 6 or 8 Calashes — we went
to Mass house — then to see the Falls then took a Walk — [*came home
abt. 6 When the Indians were pleasd to fav.r us with a grand Dance — we
returnd home abt. 8 —*]

16th

Rose early this Morning took a Ride to the Celebrated Sellere [*16th 2d.
Breakfast at Wilcocks took a ride to Sillere breakf — walk round the Town.
Dind wt. Harrison supp'd with D & Lees*][102] A most beautiful Road all the

---

[101]Edward Harrison (ca. 1729–94), merchant, shipowner, seigneur, office holder, associated with
the merchants Dobie and Ermatiger; *Dictionary of Canadian Biography* 4:329–31; accessed at <http://
www.biographi.ca/en/index.php>.

[102]Sillery, the name of Canada's first Indian reserve and one of the country's earliest Jesuit seigneuries,
located just west of old Quebec City.

Way — here we were honord with the Co. of Miss Fermos & several other of the Choralers of Emily[103] — we returned home took a 2d. Breakfast with Wilcocks took a Walk to see some of the publick Buildings came to Harrisons where we din'd broke up from Table 8 O Clock — supd wt. D. & Lees left at 11

17th

Breakfasted at Harrisons [*17th 3d Breakf. Harrisons, dind at Grants Sup'd at Davidson & Lees*] took a Walk to see the Garden Fort &c. din'd at Grants from whence with great Difficulty we got abt. 5 O Clock — we suppd with Davidson & Lees —

18

Breakf.d with Wilcocks [*18t 4t Breakfd Wilcocks dind D & Lee supd at home — Plains of Abrama (Abraham) Mt. Pleasant — Wolf Cove*] din'd with went to view the Town & at 11 Clock we did ourselves the hr. to wait on the Gov.r [Carleton] who gave us a very gentel Reception & a pressing Invitation to dine with him, but being engad every Day we were excusd — we din'd wt. Co. at Das & Lees & forrm'd a Party to take a Ride — went to Silleri, Wolfs Cove[104] — returnd by Plains of Abraham & Drank tea ^coffee^ at a house on the top of Queb. Hill where Gentlemen walk out almt every Day — here is the fin.t Propect in the World

19th 5—

Breakfd Mt. Pleas.t went to Abrams Height — with Moreland, dind at home set off after taking leave of many of our Acq.t & some of whom accompanied us abt 9 Mile out of town where we took a part.g Glass to them & to Quebeck — we road 18 Mile further when we took up our Lodging in Co. wt. Ermantinger —

---

[103]Perhaps intending "Choraleers of Émile" or "Choraleers of Saint-Émile."
[104]Wolfe's Cove, formerly Anse au Foulon, on the St. Lawrence River a short distance above Quebec City.

20th

Rose at 5 order'd our Calashes rode on abt. 9 Mile mounted [letter illegible] got to 3 Rivers abt. Dusk eat Supper ———— &c.

21st

Went to see the several [word illegible] & Manufacture here sat off at 11 O Clock — dind on some Bread & Beef &, got to N. Corp abt. 5 O Clock parted with [word illegible]

22nd

Set off our horses to [word illegible] to meet us at [word illegible] cross'd the St. Laurence at Berier[105] — the People at Mass we could not get Calashes for some time — got on to Sam.l Jacobs[106] to Dinner the finest Part of Canada all improvfd by the beautiful River Chamblea [Chambly] had by him 26000 Bush of Wheat & has sold 24000 this Summer — Got to a little hut where we lodgd

23rd

Rose very early got on to Chamblea fort[107] — breakf.d wt. the Com. Officer — got a Cart of a curious Construction & got to St. Johns abt 1 O Clock staid where we were overtak'd by Cap Fairchild & Reeves & of New York &c. J Mercer of Quebeck with whom we engaged to set of the next Mor.g

24!

This Morn.g abt. 10 O Clock sat of in a batteau wch. springing a leak we were oblig'd to put to got — a kings Boat & came on to a boat of

---

[105] Possibly intending Berthier, present-day Berthierville on the north side of the St. Lawrence River midway between Trois-Rivières and Montreal at Ile St-Ignace.

[106] Samuel Jacobs (d. 1786) was a wealthy merchant who for many years operated a variety of business enterprises along the Richelieu River; *Dictionary of Canadian Biography* 4:384–86; accessed at <http://www.biographi.ca/en/index.php>.

[107] Fort Chambly, at the foot of the Chambly Rapids on the Richelieu River, was built in 1711. Now a Canadian National Historic Site.

Mercers — abt. 2 O Clock we got out of Chamblea din'd on board the wind dying rowd on got abt. 50 Mile supd & slept on board in our G Coats with the heavens for our Canopy

25

Put of early — Champlain appeared beautiful — got abt. 40 Mile — breakf.d din'd sup'd & slept on board —

26

Set of early this Morning got to C Point to Dinner — Crown Fort[108] — 1/2 a Mile on dind then got to Ticonderoga at 8 O Clock at Night —

27

Walkd to Lake George Land.g got on board & saild over in a Pirreau [pirogue] 36 Miles in abt. 5 hours, din'd at Ft. George[109] raind — Romanticky Mountain & staid all N. Ft. George —

---

[108] Fort Crown Point, built at the narrows of Lake Champlain in 1759 by British forces under the command of Jeffrey Amherst.

[109] Fort George, built in 1755 as a base for Jeffrey Amherst, was just east of contemporaneous Fort William Henry on Lake George. It was taken by patriot forces in 1775 and then abandoned in the face of General John Burgoyne's advance in 1777.

VOLUME FOUR

Canada &c.

JMF

Vol IV

1773

	Miles
Brot. forw'd	
first Tavern	14
Stone house	14
Breakf. Tav.n	11
[Great] Barrington	14
Chadocks	9
Springs	7
Glacow [Glasgow]	11
Westfield	11
Springfield	8
Chappels	5
Graves	9
Bloomfield [Brookfield]	16
~~Graves~~ ^Spencer^	9
Lucertes [Leicester]	5
Worcester	6
Shrew[s]bury	6
Northbury	5
Marlborough	9
Sudbury	8
Bro.t forw'd	
Waterton [Watertown]	12
Boston	10
Jamaica Lake, Camb.) & back) }	20
Neawak	12
Piedmont	12
Ipswich	12
Newbury	11
Ambsbury [Amesbury]	4
Noltons	10
Portsmouth [N.H.]	10

Castle & back	4
Newbury	20
^Green Woods^	
Ipswich	11
Belerby [Beverly]	11
Salem	1
Marblehead	4
Lynn	8
Boston	12

Aug. 31st

Abt. 10 O Clock left Albany cross'd the Ferry the Road being little us'd procur'd a Guide — din'd abt. 14 Miles off on such things as we could get — x. x. x. got to a Place call'd Stone house where we lodg'd —

Sept. 1st.

Rose early sat out breakfasted abt. 11 Miles — din'd at [Great] Barrington Lodg'd at Capt. Springs — Lakes & Road & ... x.

2nd.

Rose at 5 mounted at 6. Breakf. at Glascow[110] — misbl. Roads — hill of Stone — din'd at Westfield — came thro Springfield cross'd Connecticut River 1/2 mile over — bated [baited, ate?] 5 Miles further on — Lodge 9 further at Graves

Sept.6 3d.

Breakfasted at Bloomfield [Brookfield] ^16 Miles^ — came thro Spencer 9 Miles off — din'd at Lecester [Leicester] — 5 Miles — past Worcester & Shrewsbury lodg'd at Northbury

---

[110]Glasgow is a reference to lands and a settlement a short distance from Westfield, Mass., in the direction of Blandford, where there was a tavern; Sumner Gilbert Wood, *The Taverns and Turnpikes of Blandford, 1733–1833* (Published by the author, 1908), 5, 10, 13–14.

4th.

came thro Marlborough, breakf at Sudbury — din'd at Waterton [Watertown] & got to Boston abt. 4 O Clock

5th

Went to Meetg 20 with ourselves din'd at home Coffee house Dranke tea took a Walk to the Mall when the Sun is no soon sat then it is all alive wth. Strollers —

6th

Waited on the Gentlemen to whom we had Letters din'd wth. Rowe[111] took a Walk after dinner to see the Artillery Review — drank tea at George's — [letters crossed out] took a Walk sup'd at home —

7th

Breakfasted with Thos. Aylwin[112] went to see Co: house Fanul [Faneuil] Hall, Assembly Room — Churches the Paintings of [blank] T M & Usen. — also of — [blank] went to Charlestown — hird horses to go to Cambrige Library — 114 Schol' — Build & Museum — Gifts &c. came home ^back^ dind wt. him. spent Eveng at home —

---

[111] Possibly John Rowe (1715–87), a leading merchant and major landholder in Boston.

[112] Thomas Aylwin (1729–91), a merchant and justice of the peace in Quebec City who lived in Boston from about 1769–75, where he married; *Dictionary of Canadian Biography* 4:37–38; accessed at <http://www.biographi.ca/en/index.php>.

8th.

took a Walk to view town din'd wt. Bourne[113] — went wt. S [word illegible] to see Mall — watched &c. & _____ drank tea wt. Geyer[114] spent Ev.g at home

9th.

After Breakf.t took a Ride in a Sulkey to Jamaica Pond Cambridge dind — E J at home —

10th.

Din'd wt. Aylwin in Co. wt. Geyer Roach[115] & Several G.n ~~drank~~ took a Walk to Ct. house to see Judgement on a Crim.l Judge Oliver[116] — Drank tea same Place — Ladies — Cushing — spent the Evg w. Jarvis[117] —

11th.

Breakfasted at home, waited on by sev.l Gentlemen who came to the ferry where we cross'd — Excellence of ferry — mounted abt. 1/2 pas 9 — bated [?] at [letters crossed out] Lyn[n] a pretty Vil: 12 Miles Din'd at Dansby — drank Coffee at Ipswich — a pretty Vil: abt. 200 house —

[113]Perhaps one of several loyalist Bourn brothers in Sandwich who were directed to leave the colony under the 1788 Banishment Act of Massachusetts, a bill of attainder whose purpose was, in part: "to prevent the return to this state of certain persons therein named and others who have left this state or either of the United States, and joined the enemies thereof." See Lorenzo Sabine, *Biographical Sketches of Loyalists of the American Revolution, with an Historical Essay by Lorenzo Sabine*, 2 vols. (Boston: Little, Brown, 1864), 1:241.

[114]Possibly Frederick William Geyer (d. 1803), a Boston merchant and loyalist who was among those subject to the Banishment Act; ibid., 468.

[115]This may be a reference to Francis Rotch (1750-1822), the owner of the *Dartmouth*, one of three ships involved in the Boston Tea Party, which would take place on Dec. 13, 1773; see ibid., 507.

[116]Peter Oliver (1731–791), a prominent Bostonian and loyalist, at the time chief justice of the colony of Massachusetts. He was one of the justices hearing the case of the 1770 Boston Massacre. In 1776 he entered self-exile, first to Nova Scotia and then to England, where he later died. See Gaspee Virtual Archives, <http://www.gaspee.org/Commissioners.html #Oliver>.

[117]This may be Dr. Charles Jarvis who became a delegate to the Massachusetts Ratifying Convention. Harold C. Syrett and Jacob E. Cooke, eds., *The Papers of Alexander Hamilton*, vol. 19 (New York: Columbia University Press, 1973), 129.

Indian town — got to Newbury at Dusk — waited on the C.m to whom we had letters — sup'd at home, on our Pass? we were stopd by a Man to be smoakd —

12.

Breakf.d at Newbury wh. Capt. holland[118] waited on by Jackson to go to Meet.g went home wh. him dind in Co. wt Dr. Tyler. Lowell & several others — Afternoon went to Church drank tea with Cap. Weir — took a Walk round the town stopt by a G.n wt. 8 foot cod spent Ev.g wt. Tracy — Newbury. Situation — Vessels Wharfs — 600 houses — 4 Churches Stillhouses — R — W: Indies

13th

Rose early Next Morn.g accompanied by Dr. Tyler &c J. Tracy, we set out row'd along Merrymack [Merrimac] River a great Vessels on Stockes — cross'd a ferry & breakfasted at Ambury [Amesbury] — where a late hurricane has done some minor this [word illegible] a little Vill: of Salisbury at this Place 80 Vessel are annually built — breakd here got 5 Miles further on took leave of Dr. Tyler & J. Tracy & got to Portsmouth to Dinner — waited on Gn. to whom we had Letters — spent Ev.g at house wt. Capt: J: Langdon[119] & Col: G: Boyd[120] —

14!

After Breakfast calld on by Clap[121] & Langdon took a Walk round town — 800 house wood laid out — situation — River Capt. N. Hampshire — Vessels built — 33 now — 60 an: Peninsula — Wharfs — Gen dine wt.

---

[118]Possibly Richard Holland, subject to the 1788 Banishment Act of Massachusetts. See Sabine, *Biographical Sketches,* 1: 538.

[119]Capt. J. Langdon is John Langdon (1741–1819), merchant, shipbuilder, Revolutionary War general, signer of the Constitution, and three-term governor of New Hampshire.

[120]George Boyd (d. 1787), a prominent merchant and shipbuilder in Portsmouth.

[121]This might be Supply Clap or Clapp (1742–1811), a resident of Portsmouth.

Col: Boyd King Cleveland Wandel[122] Sherbury & &c &c. — supd wt. Cleveland Langdon &c.

15th

Breakf.d on Co. 3 Brothers Capt. Cleveland — wt. with Capt. King & Langdon to Fort[123] — pretty Fortification — on the Entrance of River — sea Side Cannon — Run.g Harbourd tide dind wth. Meshan the Collector spent the Ev.g on a Party where 29 Ld. & Gn. were present broke up at 2 O Clock & went on board there where we supp'd got home at 3 —

16th

Breakfasted wt. Cap: holland [word illegible] Genl. w his curious Collection of original [words illegible] for a May of great Extent — din'd wh. his Excellency Gov.r Wentworth[124] — Capt holland — Trail — Gen Lady supd with Trail — Cleveland [word illegible] — drank tea wh. Sheaf[125]

17th

at 6 O Clock calld on by Langdon — ^Sheaf^ Boyd & Clap — Who accompanied 5 Mile to Breakfast where we parted — dind at Newby at Tracy's — accompanied by R Tracy — Coffin & out of Respect —as far as Salem where we lay —

---

[122]Possibly John Wendell (1731–1808), a prominent Portsmouth land holder and conveyancer who was connected to a number of important figures of the Revolution, including Hamilton, Jay, Hancock, and others. See James Rindge Stanwood, *The Direct Ancestry of the Late Jacob Wendell* . . . . Boston: David Clapp and Son, 1882), 27.

[123]Fort William and Mary, the only active military installation in Portsmouth at this time, was located on a point of land on New Castle Island (town of New Castle); Jeremy Belknap, *The History of New Hampshire* . . . ., vol. 2 (Dover: O. Crosby and J. Varney, 1812), 289, names Captain John Langdon as a leader of a large party of anti-British citizens who raided the fort in mid-December 1774, seizing the supply of munitions there.

[124]John Wentworth (1737–1820), British colonial governor of New Hampshire.

[125]Possibly Jacob Sheafe (d. 1791), a local merchant who had interests in several ships sailing out of Portsmouth.

18th

Parted wh. them — took a walk round the Town — harbour Vessels Fisheres — regulant newness — of houses — Wharfs &c. & breakfasted — & got to ~~Lyn to din~~ Marblehead fine harbour — 60 Vessel at Anchor — no tide — Flake of Fishes — Romanticy we got to Lyn to Dine & to Boston at 5 O Clock

19th

Waited on ~~early~~ this Morn.g by Gey[er]. who accompanied us to Baptist M.g where Stillman[126] preach'd to the Crim.l under Sentence of D.th dind w.th him where were [blank] afternoon went to hear Dr. Cooper[127] — drank tea wih Dr. Lean — took a Walk to a Mall & spent Ev.g at home —

~~19th~~ 20th

Breakfasted wh. T. Aylwin went wt. Roach to ~~view~~ see the celebrated Poetess ~~Ph~~ Miss Phillis Wheatly[128] who had but just returned from England — where she had been much caress'd — she shew'd us t a Vol: of her Poetry which ~~are~~ ^is^ shortly to appear in Print & a Number of her Letters sensible & din'd wh. Roach in Co. wth P: Hughs & some other Gent — After Dinner wth Capt: Prince[129] Hughs Roach & sev.l other went on board a Seventy four Gun Ship commanded by Adm.l Montagu[130] where we were treated wh. great Civility drank tea &c. &c. &c. _____

---

[126] The Reverend Samuel Stillman (1737–1807), minister of the First Baptist Church of Boston, a founding trustee of what is today Brown University and a member of the Massachusetts Senate Convention for the adoption of the 1788 Constitution.

[127] Perhaps the Reverend Samuel Cooper (1725–1783), a prominent and respected minister in Boston.

[128] Poet Phillis Wheatley (1753–84), a native of present-day Senegal and a former slave, the first published African-American poet, then living in Boston. Her famous work, *Poems on Various Subjects, Religious and Moral,* was published in 1773, the year of Fisher's journey. See Vincent Carretta, *Phyllis Wheatley: Biography of a Genius in Bondage* (Athens: University of Georgia Press, 2011).

[129] Possibly Samuel Prince, banished by the 1788 Act.

[130] The Royal Navy's Admiral John Montagu (1719–95), Commander-in-Chief of the North American station and enforcer of the Crown's Boston Port Act, which would be enacted in response to the Boston Tea Party.

sup'd wth T: Cuishg[131] — wife & ————

[scribbles] 21t

Accompanied by Geyer, Wife, & Polly Ingeam, we set out from Boston, breakfasted at the Peacock — din'd at 13 Miles dist' Wentham [Wrentham], got to Providence at 8 in the Eav where we met wth our old Compn; Mercer we reced an Invitation to spend the Evening wh a Party of Ladies — [word illegible] refusd —

22st

After Breakfs went to view To. Aqudents[132] — ^Moulbon^[133] 700 houses — improv'd fast — grow.g Place — dined home, went to Point Grove, lover Leap — &c in Aftn went to drinke tea wh [letter illegible] Boyen[134] & Sister — Carlus[135] & several — others — Capt: Gregaire & c &c — spent Evng. wh. them

23d —

After Breakfast ~~went~~ took leave of our Frds. got to Rk? to Dinner — cros'd B ferys & reachd N Port abt. 5 O Clock — waited on by Dr. Easton[136] went in the Evng to Maulbons & the Robinsons[137] sup'd at home — Prospects &c

---

[131] Thomas Cushing (1725–88), an attorney and statesman from Boston and a delegate to the Continental Congress.

[132] Intending Aquidneck, as in Aquidneck Island, on which Newport is located.

[133] The home of Francis Malbone (d. 1791), a prosperous trader in Newport. His son, Francis Malbone, Jr. (1759–1809), was later a representative and senator from Rhode Island. A portrait of Francis and his brother Saunders was painted by Gilbert Stuart about 1773.

[134] Fisher may have heard Bowen, possibly Jabez Bowen (1739–1815), a member of the Providence town council who was involved in the shipping trade, including the importation of slaves.

[135] Perhaps George Corlis, a ship owner from Providence, RI.

[136] This may be Jonathan Easton (1747–1813), a member of the notable Easton family, the patriarch of which, Nicholas (1593–1675), was a founder of Newport and served three terms as Rhode Island's president (governor).

[137] There was a Robinson family in Newport who were Quakers.

24

Breakfasted at home, dind at Jn. Wanton's;[138] viewed town, drank tea at P. Clarks[139] — went to Library — build.g Synagogue[140] sup'd wh. J Wanton —

25th

Called on by J. Wanton to take a Ride to Purgatory,[141] white Hall &c. Fishing — Beach — came to dinner w! T. Robinson drank tea wh. B. Gadwin & others — spent Evng wth. Ellory[142] who mt. the fam'd Geo. at A Redwood[143] wh. J Clark[144] & Wife _____

26!

Went to Meeting, din'd w. Dr. Easton to Meetg, again, drank tea wh. P. Clark, took a Walk wh. Gladwin[,] Thurston[145] &c & supd wh. T. Robinson —

27 —

T Wt Dr. Easton — P. Robinson, Ph. Robinson B: Thurston — Th: Lawton, Sister, Gladwin &c took a Ride to Redwoods Garden call'd at

---

[138] There were several persons named John of the prominent Wantons of Newport, a Quaker family. However, this may be John G. Wanton (1729–99), a successful merchant and the son of former Rhode Island colonial governor Gideon Wanton (1745–46). See John Russell Bartlett, *History of the Wanton Family of Newport, Rhode Island* (Providence: Sidney and Rider, 1878).

[139] Possibly Peleg Clarke, a Newport merchant and operator of a slave brokerage. He later served as alderman.

[140] The Tuoro Synagogue, completed in 1763, the oldest synagogue in the United States.

[141] Today, Purgatory Chasm, a naturally formed deep crevice in the rock ledges east of Easton Bay.

[142] This may be William Ellery (1727–1820), naval officer, politician, attorney, and signer of the Declaration of Independence.

[143] Abraham Redwood (1709/10–88), a founder of the Company of the Redwood Library in Newport in 1747, leading to the establishment of the Redwood Library and Athenæum, the oldest lending library in the United States.

[144] A John or Jonathan Clark who was banished by the 1788 Act.

[145] There was a Gardner Thurston (1721–1802), who served as Newport's baptist minister.

Whitehall[146] din'd on Turtle spent the Afternoon & return'd home in the Evng —

28th.

Breakf. wh J: Wanton, took a Ride to So: ferry took leave of our Fr'd B: not without some Reflections thence to L: house — return'd home cros'd the ferry 3 M: wide in 20 Minute going — & 15 coming — din'd wh. Ellery at Redwoods took a Ride wh. Clark & him to Bowlers Garden[147] — 4 Ac: Eas. side of Island. Prospect of the River &c Images. Summer house — spent Evng & sup'd at Jos: Clarks —

29th

Breakfasted at home, to Court din'd early & took a Ride to Maulbon's Garden, large Birch all burnt. Garden — Fishpond —Tommony hill[148] — Avenue — drank tea wt. B Gl — Evng at home —

30th

Breakfasted at home, went to Court, din'd wt. Fran: Maulbon went to Redwood Library — elegant Building — 1500 Vol: 13 by R: Lot by Collins — Pictures of those Benefactors — spent Evng at P. Lawton —

October 1

Breakfasted with Ellory. went to Court. Lawy. Juste. [letters illegible] din'd with John Wanton, dranke tea at Thurstons. spent Evn.g at Robinson

---

[146] The home of George Berkeley (1685–1753), Anglican priest, philosopher, and educator, in Newport. Here met a literary and philosophical discussion group that was the forerunner of the Redwood Library.

[147] At the home of Metcalf Bowler (1726–89), a prosperous merchant, shipowner, judge, and politician residing in Newport.

[148] Tomony Hill (infrequently Tammany Hill), a high point of land near the Malbone home at Newport Harbor. It allegedly was the scene of an execution in 1696. See John Ross Dix, *A Hand-book of Newport and Rhode Island* (Newport: C. E. Hammett, Jr., 1852), 142–43; Edward Peterson, *History of Rhode Island and Newport* (New York: John S. Taylor, 1853), 60.

Octr 2nd

Din'd with A: Redwood, took a Ride to Farm wt. Ellory — Brother Clark
— evng. at Robinsons —

Octr 3rd

Breakfasted at Clarks — din'd at J: Wantons — ~~sup~~ tea & sup'd wt. T.
Robinsons —
[Jabez Maud Fisher's journal ends here]

Appendix 1

Editors' note: The lyrics below—one of several versions of the undated traditional French sailor's song, "*La Femme du Président*" ("The President's Wife")—are not in Fisher's hand. They appear in his journal following the entry for August 5.

[line illegible]
[words illegible] <u>un beau</u>
[word illegible] <u>est si parfait en beauté</u>
<u>Qu'Une dame a su charmé</u>
<u>Beau marinier, beau marinier</u>
<u>Madame voudrais bien vous parlér</u>
<u>Beauté</u>
<u>Allez y vite & promptement</u>
<u>Car c'est la femme d'un president</u>
<u>Le marinier s'en est allé, ^Le si^ s'en est allé</u>
<u>D'roit au jardin des oliviers</u>
~~pour voir~~ <u>^Trouva^ la femme du president</u>
<u>Un dub aisér lui fait present</u>
<u>Beau marinier &c</u>
<u>Aujourd'hui as tu dejeuné</u>
<u>Beauté</u>
<u>Montons dans ma chambrette montons</u>
<u>Nous y ferons collation</u>
<u>La collation qu'ils ont fait, le collation qu'ils ont fait</u>
<u>Il a duré trois jours & trois nuits, il a duré trois jours &c</u>
<u>Trois jours & trois nuits il passa son tems</u>
<u>Avec la femme du President</u>
<u>Le marinier s'est enn^u^ye, le marinier s'est ennuye</u>
<u>Par la fenetre a regarde</u>
<u>Madame donnez moi mon congée</u>
<u>Les vents sont bons pour m'embarquer</u>
<u>Beau marinier &c beau marinier</u>

[word crossed out] De moi ne vas point mal parlé
Voila cent ecu d'ors comtés
Sera pour boire a ma santé
Le marinier s'en (fut) ^vat^ abord
Le marinier &c
[words illegible] d'or
Enfans buvons a la santé
D'une dame que j'ai su charmé
Il est cau^c^au le president
Et moi J'emporte son argent

[Translation]

[line illegible]
[words illegible] a handsome
[word illegible] is such a perfect beauty
That a woman did woo
Handsome mariner, handsome mariner
Madame would like to speak to you
Beauty
Go there quick, make haste
For 'tis the president's wife
The mariner went on his way, went on his way
Straight to the olive grove
To see the president's wife
A sweet kiss he gave her
Handsome mariner
Today have you breakfasted
Beauty
Up to my room let us go
We shall take refreshment there
The refreshment they took, the refreshment they took
Lasted three days and three nights
Three days and three nights he spent his time
With the president's wife
The mariner grew restless, the mariner grew restless,
Out the window he did gaze
Madame let me take my leave
The winds are fair to join my ship

Handsome mariner, handsome mariner,
Pray do not speak ill of me
Here are one hundred gold écus'
To drink to my health
The mariner went aboard
The mariner, etc.
[Words illegible] gold
Boys, let's drink to the health
Of a lady I wooed
The president has horns
And with his money I came away

Appendix 2

Editors' note: What follows is Fisher's narrative on the Indians he encountered on his travels. It appears in his journal after the entry for August 5 and the French-language song in Appendix 1. Most of what Fisher offers echoes what is found in a number of other mid- to late eighteenth-century accounts of the native people of the region. His descriptions of Indian dress and physical appearance, however, are especially informative.[149] It is nonetheless likely, especially when the details Fisher provides on leadership and decision-making are considered, that much of his information came from others, perhaps the military personnel he visited or knowledgeable persons with whom he spoke while at Akwesasne (St. Regis) and Kahnawake (Caughnawaga) on the St. Lawrence River. It is also possible that Fisher obtained some of his information from published accounts he had read after his return, perhaps writing his narrative at that point.

In their Speeches they deal much in Allegories & Metaphors, & their Comparisons are remarkably striking & applicable. they are spirited bold unconfus'd, will speak hours together without being at a loss — tho they never speak till they are Masters of the Subject —
Their Cabbins how built — their Canoes, their Manner of dealing — [.]
They will divide it amongst them — & I have been told by a Gentleman of Credit, who hav.g often had Occasion to give them Rum &c. has sometimes done it in Mugs, which they have immediately drank — & when one has imagin'd he has taken more than his Share, he has call'd another & spirted out of his own mouth such Part as he thought he had

---

[149]See, generally, Warren Johnson, "Journal" of Warren Johnson." In *In Mohawk Country: Narratives of a Native People*, eds. Dean R. Snow, Charles T. Gehring, and William A. Starna (Syracuse: Syracuse University Press, 1996), 250–73 [1760–61]; Joseph Bloomfield, "Journal of Joseph Bloomfield." In *In Mohawk Country*, 274–91 [1776]; François-Jean de Beauvoir, Marquis de Chastellux. "Visit to Schenectady, 1780." In *In Mohawk Country*, 292–94 [1780]; Peter Sailly, "Diary of Peter Sailly on a Journey in American in the Year 1784." In *In Mohawk Country*, 295–99 [1784]; François Marbois, "Journey to the Oneidas, 1784." In *In Mohawk Country*, 300–17 [1784]; Cesare Marino and Karim M. Tiro, eds. and trans., *Along the Hudson and Mohawk: The 1790 Journey of Count Paolo Andreani* (Philadelphia: University of Pennsylvania Press, 2006); Paolo Adreani, "Travels of a Gentleman from Milan." In *In Mohawk Country* [1790]. Also on Indian dress, see Timothy Shannon, "Dressing for Success on the Mohawk Frontier: Hendrick, William Johnson, and the Indian Fashion." *William and Mary Quarterly* 53, no. 1 (1996): 13–42.

more into the Mouth of his Brother who made no Scruple of rec.g it in
that manner — They are too remarkably charitable to all in Distress &
will often give of the last Morsel they have in the World to a Stranger
without looking to the next Day what they are to do for themselves this
however is a want of Oeconomy which cannot altogether be justified —
But as they have no Idea of Individual Property, but every thing in
common among them is may be accounted for — & this makes them
look on the whites as sordid & mean to a very great Degree, in acquiring
Wealth & not dissipating the necessaries of Life among those whose
necessity demands it — & this is their Argument whenever they plunder
which is not at all uncommon as a man cannot drive a Herd of Sheep or
Cattle thro their Lands without losing one or more, which they will do in
his Sight & bid him Defiance. They are very fond of smoak.g are very
ingenious in making their pipes which are prettily carv'd out of Stones of
different kinds & Colors — They cannot often procure Tobacco, as a
Substitute they make use of either the Shumack [sumac] or sweet Grass
the latter of which is particularly aromatic & very grateful, & is thought
wholsome. They have many very curious Secrets in the Article of
Physic & Disorders to which their Constitutions are particularly Subject
they cure with less Difficulty more Certainty & less time than the whites
— Inflamable Soars & Hurts in [word crossed out] Fevers &c. They
likewise know many Roots which dye very admirably well — but of these
as well as well as their Secrets in Physic they religiously adhere to keep
among themselves[.]
Dress Canoes fast Comparisons in the [words illegible] fishing.
The Dress of the Men —
They wear a great Part of their Head bald, the hind Part of most of it
being brought up to the Crown it is there ty'd with a String ornamented
with Beads, & generally something hanging down from it, their hair is
black as jet. Their Ears they cut great gashes in & by hanging Weights by
Degrees it at length hangs down a great Distance — in wh. they are very
proud of wearing any taudry jingling Ornament I saw one who had a long
streak cut of from each Ear & being bound together had grown as
perfectly to each other as if they had been united at Origine — their faces
they are very fond of painting, with great Blotches & Streaks of red they
cut monstrous scars in their Flesh, & have many drawing which have a
blue Stain but this signification they do not want known —[.]
They use a great Quantity of Bears Grease wt. which they daub their
hair & body, which makes the Sun the less effect them — they wear a

Cloth wh. comes under their Thighs & is tyd round their waist by a Belt
— some of them in the Summer & all of them in the Winter wear
Leggings — & some of wh. are ornamented with Beads &c. they have
Mockinsons, made of Buckskins but without Ornament unless on a
particular Occasion [*Breast & Arm Plates &c*] — the above & a Blanket
compleats their Dress, except a Shirt & this only a few of them wear,
they are either Leather or coarse Linnin which they put on & never wash,
or scarce ever pull off till it is wore out — The Women all wear their hair
ty'd & hang.g down behind either in a Tin, Silver or Brass Case, or a bag
of Beads — or heedlessly flow.g in shining Ringlets behind them, they
mostly wear a shirt, wh. is most frequently ornamented with as many
Broaches as they can procure — they have short Petticoats com.g just
below their knees, & are bare leg'd & footed during the Warm months —
they have a Blanket over them & if they have Children they have a Belt
which goes Round their waist — & the blanket hanging behind them
with a Child in it is upheld by a Tompline round their Foreheads — if
thev have no Children they carry their Burthens in this Manr. Their
Children while suckl.g are tied to a board, with Blankets swaddled round
it — & are never releas'd an hour together from their Prison after they
pass this stage being which they are repeated dip'd in cold Water to
harden them, they go in Summer Months naked as our first Parents
——[.]

Their travelling is either in Canoes or on Foot, tho' some of them have
latterly got to keeping horses on which they bring their Furrs to Market
— on foot they will travel a great Way in a Day — especially when they
hunt — in their Canoes they travel very fast, with two Paddles they will
go faster than a Batteau with 4 Oars of this we had repeated Instances —
tho sometimes I have seen 6 or 8 of them paddle at a time ——[.]

Bodies of their Dead, regard The Indians ^live^ for the most part in little
Villages of their own their houses consist chiefly of little Huts of but one
Appartment & that very dirty — ~~Tho~~ The men are fond of strolling much
abroad they live chiefly by hunting except a few Individuals who have of
late years gott a little into the Cultivation of Agriculture whatever furrs
they get they immediately go with to the whites & barter for such Goods
as they use which are little besides Blankets Paints Beads Toys & Rum of
which last they are very fond & will always drink to excess if they can
procure it at any moderate Rates, tho indeed to do Justice to the Traders,
so great a Regard have they for the Welfare of their Healths that so far
back as Niagara they sell it at no less than 12/p Gallon & in this is just a

considerable Quantity of Water color'd with Saffron one ~~would~~ of the traders being challeng'd with put.g in 9 Gall: of Water to one of Rum declared ~~of~~ he never put in but 7 — one would imagine from these Circumstances the Indians would defer dealing in an Article so prejudicial, yet so great is their Love for it, that at the Expence of their health & their old Age, they will never refuse it, & take every measure to procure it, which when they have not wherewith to purchase they will beg it of any Body —[.]

The Women have particularly experienced a Barrenness since the Introduction of the Article among them & cases are not seldom that when they have been drunk they have destroy'd their own Children — ^this inpacts differently on them^[.] Their Standing Food is Indian Corn, which they all raise in greater or lesser Quantity & whenever they go abroad they take some of this with them, which they Cook & eat with great Avidity, tho they live most principally on this, yet in the Spring & Summer Months they do not want for Variety, they have on almost all the principle Creeks or Rivers where there are any Falls Eel Wares [weirs] which are made Viz. & these great Number resort, & build themselves Wigwams in which they reside 2 or 3 Months, as their Success may be, these Fish as they very much abound in all their Creeks, they take such Quantities of, as by smoaking them properly will serve them near the whole Year, of this they are very fond, they likewise catch considerable Numbers of ^Catfish^ Salmon & Bass, tho they know nothing yet abt. Hook & Line, this is all done by Spears which they dart with amazing Dexterity & scarce ever fail of hitting their Prey — They have besides Guns wth. which they shoot some Game, a Palate Gun with which they blow a wooden Spear a considerable Distance,[150] with nice Accuracy & since they lost the Art of Bow & Arrow they use these in lieu — & got many little Birds by it — they likewise make Traps for Bears Wolves Otters &c. of which they are fond & their Skins are valuable — They never make Presents but with an Expectation of receiv.g an Equivalent — an Instance whereof I could but remark, some of the Ottowaws gave us some smoak'd Eels, & soon after asked for some ^Rum^ & on being

---

[150]This description of a blowgun—Fisher's "palate gun"—is the earliest known mention of this game weapon anywhere in the historic record from northeastern North America. It is believed to have reached the Iroquois via one of the southern Iroquoian-speaking groups; William N.Fenton, *The Great Law and the Longhouse: A Political History of the Iroquois Confederacy* (Norman: University of Oklahoma Press, 1998), 10; Carroll L. Riley, "The Blowgun in the New World." *Southwestern Journal of Anthropology* 8, no. 3 (1952): 309, 315.

inform'd we had none, without much Ceremony they took back the
Eels & went off — they have not in their Language any Words which
convey an Idea of Trust —[.]

Their Constitution is uncertain & unfixt they have a king for each
Nation, & whenever any Warrior makes himself famous for a remarkable
Achievement a Number will attatch themselves to him give him a
Name, & this Party are known ^as a Tribe^ by the Name ~~they give him~~
^he may chuse,^ as a Bear they will all go this Name of the Bear Tribe so
with Wolf, Fox, Otter, Alligator Porcupine &c.[151] always observ.g to give
him a Name somewhat applicable & more or less honorable accordg to
the greatness of the Act they may have perform'd ^some Nations have 20
Tribes^ — Their king except in War or Council has very little Deference
paid him, his Appearance would not distinguish him as being better, but
generally worse as in order to keep up his Authority & Weight he is
oblig'd to give Presents to considerable Amt. & not having any annual
Income they are generally poor. They have a Number Sagems [sachems]
or Wisemen who act as Counsellors These are compos'd of old
experienced Warriors, whom have laid by all pretensions from their Age
to excel in their Art — these are always first consulted on any Occasion
of Consequence, & if they apprehend they are ever aggreiv'd these first
endeavour to bring abt. a Reconciliation, if these however fail then come
in the Warriors Men ambitious of Glory in this & who generally are most
desirous of War, Then with threats have often brought abt. Matters when
other Measures have fail'd — Their Women have not a little to do with
Government, on the Death of a king as the Crown is not absolutely
hereditary, they chuse a new one, & are by no Means oblig'd to award it
to the Son of the late one but as they may think his merit entitles him
—[.]

They have a Council to of their own, & ~~have~~ ^are^ always consulted in
Peace or War & in some Instances when a Peace has been concluded on
by the Male, the female Government have totally set their Intentions aside
by upbraiding the Men with Cowardice an Epithet they of all others the

---

[151] Rather than "tribes," Fisher may be attempting to describe "clans," although the alligator is
geographically out of place. Nonetheless, the presence of the blowgun mentioned before demonstrates
a link to the southeast where there were alligator clans—in particular among the Seminoles. Moreover,
although it plays a minor role and its time depth is unknown, there is an alligator dance in the ceremonial
repertoire of the Iroquois; see Gertrude Prokosch Kurath, *Iroquois Music and Dance: Ceremonial Arts of
Two Seneca Longhouses* (Bureau of American Ethnology Bulletin 187. Washington, DC: U. S. Government
Printing Office), 1964.

most detest & abhor, & coming from a Woman is an Argument doubly armd —[.]

Their Children are brought up with the Love of War —[.]

As to their Religion they seem to have very little Idea of any at all They all acknowledge a Deity, & a number of Lesser or tutelar ones, the one presides over the Lesser & the lesser over particular Objects they have a God of hunting as well as of War, & if in war they fail they suppose their God of War is angry with them, if in hunting they fail of Success they suppose their

~~Meteriological Observations From New York to~~ [152] God of hunting is angry & will often offer to appease him, by addressing in the Shape of a Tree a Stone &c. — they have some Idea of Futurity, which I cannot better describe than by the following Anecdote —[:]

An Indian having in a very inhuman & barbarous manner kill'd another, when the king of the Nation came to hear of it, He address'd the dead Body in the following manner. "You have been guilty of much wrong & many Sins but for your murderers Cruelty your Sins shall all rest on him & you shall be cleansd["] — a Doctrine however absurd is certainly well calculated to put a Stop to the Effusion of so much blood —[.]

They are excessive indolent especially the Men who so long inur'd to a life of Idleness & rambling cannot bear the thought of cultivating any of the Mechanic Arts among them — the whole laborious Part that they go thro falls on the Women, who carry on the Manufacturers of such Toys as they make to dispose of to the ~~Indians~~ ^whites^, if an Indian kills a Bear or a Deer he will skin it, & if it is within 2 or 3 Mile of his house he will not himself bring it home but will send his Squaw for it knotching the Trees all the Way to it that she may be able to find it — This the good Women do not think hard of, they do it with the greatest Patience, & calmness. A Man is not limited to one or two Wives, but may take as many as he pleases, keep them as long & discard them whenever he chuses — the Children if any are generally divided between them, they are rather thought a Relief than a Burthen as their Support is easily procur'd — Their Marriages are by no means formal no other Ceremony being made use of than some trifling Present to the Father for his Daughter, who never fails complying with his Terms. The Indians tho in

---

[152]This struck out line is at the bottom of the page and inverted, suggesting that it had originally been entered as a topic heading that Fisher then abandoned.

their Nature wild fierce & savage & little regardful of their lives in
Comparison with other Nations, are great Cowards, as will appear from
this Instance — they have a Maxim among them, that it is glorious for
them to fly when they behold a greater Number in their Enemy than they
have themselves — & they are call'd rash, imprudent & look'd on
unskilful to break thro' —[.]
The Children of many of them have good Features, & the Women in
particular till after they are married are far from being disagreeable, but
the Laborious lives they afterwards lead, has such an Effect on them that
they appear as much like Montrers[153] as of the Sex they belong to — their
voices are remarkably soft & delicate —[.]
They have among all their Gross & inhuman Qualities, one [word
illegible] peculiar to themselves [word illegible] which deserves Praise
from every Body. & worthy of being follow'd — that ~~the~~ is their
Generosity wh. extends to a Degree almost beyond Credit — if a loaf of
bread or Buiscuit is given ^to^ one of them they are careful always to
divide it as exact as possible among them if 30 of them were present the
same if rum is given them, I have seen a bottle pour'd into a large
Bowl & a number of them being present ^to make the portion more
equal^ each one take a Spoon out if it holds more[.]

---

[153] Perhaps intending French *monstres* "monsters."

81

Appendix 3

Editor's note: The text that follows is from the blotter adjacent to the entry of August 9.

some of our accompanied to the Water Side. Montreal is prettily situated on the NW: side of ~~an island~~ ^the^ River on an Island at the Foot of a Mountain of the same Name — It consists principally of 2 Streets wh. run parralell with the River & are pretty strait — it is the 2.d Town in Canada for Size but the first for its Situation — & Exports — the vast trade carried on here is principally up the grande Riviere, wh. has an easy Intercourse with Lake Huron & here almost all the Furrs come down, tho some come from Detroit down the St. Lawrence & a considerable Quantity of Dry Goods are sent there, all this Trade is carried in Bark Canoes — the Amt. of Furrs sent from this Place last year Sales amt. to £100,000. the Quantity annually increases, The Wheat is very considerable it is thought this Year it will amount to 200,000 Bushells — ~~the Amt. of D~~ the greater Part of this is sent down in Sloops to Quebeck. from whence it is exported, as the Inconvenience of Sea Vessels coming up to load here is great on Acct. of the strong Current for upwards of 120 Mile below & a Vessel cannot get up without a fair & strong Wind, for which they often wait 2 or 3 Weeks ——[.]
The Land round abt. is very Luxuriant & the Wheat rais'd here is extraordinary good, the Prospects of the Country round about are scarce to be equalld — the easy manner in which lands are held are peculiar to this Country — the Land being originally granted by the King of France to such of his Subjects, as paid him certain Sums in ~~Large~~ Tracts of abt. 12 Mile by 30 — these Owners of these ~~Lands~~ ^Tracts^ into which all Canada is divided are call'd Seniors & ~~that it~~ each particular Estate is call'd a Seigniorie [seigneurie][154] — at the first grant ~~it was~~ certain terms were agree'd on for the Division of the Seniories into small Farms, wh.

---

[154] Seigneurie, scores of long, narrow strips of land laid out under the seigneurial system introduced to New France in 1626. These parcels were owned by the king of France and overseen by local landlords called seigneurs. This semi-feudal system of land holding existed legally until 1854.

were to be as easy as possible for the more speedy Settlement of the
Colony by Emigrants, the Terms were that the Land should be taken up
in Tracts of 3 arpens in front & abt. 30 Deep — at the execution of any
Deed of Conveyance the Seignior [seigneur] was to receive one Crown
french — & all the Emolument he was after to receive, was a Preference
in Case the Land was to be sold of his purchasing — & in case it was to
be sold without his Consent — he has a year & a Day in wh. time if he
pleases he may disannull the Sale — this & an Alienation fine which he
always receives on the transferring the Property from one to another in
some Estates is furnished a pretty maintenance — this Manner of
granting Lands & every Tract being of the same has naturally induc'd
every Person to take up Land in a Situation he may look on the most
eligible — & this the Reason that all the Lands on the Water from above
this Place to below Quebeck are taken up on the River — This is the
most happy Country in the World on Acct. of Taxes — there is no Tax of
any Kind, except what the Romans Pay to their Priests wh. is one tenth of
all they raise, but this is voluntary & what most of the Farmers fail of
doing as they can get Absolution for this on the same terms they do for
other Greivances. the Protestants pay no Tax at all of any kind — all the
Civil & military Expences are paid by the Government at home, wh.
amount only to abt. 12000£ Sterl.g includ.g the Salaries of all the
Governors & Council They have no Assembly & all Acts for the
^internal^ government of the Province are [word illegible] by the
Governor & Council — The People here are all upon an Equality every
Man has his portion of Land ^on wh.^ he can live support his Family,
keep his horse & Calash & every Eatable is supplied for him at a very
moderate Expence — the horses are as good as any in the World — &
they are in no place cheaper, they live long & are ^uncommonly^ hardy
— Vegetables of every kind are plenty & cheap — & any Dish of Meat
may be furnish'd at a low Price — The richest Seignior enjoys no more
he has no better Carriage than a Calash no Beast but a Canadian horse,
his Living is no better, no Luxury has yet crept in among them — the
poorest Canadian here is warmly clad — the richest is not gay — the
french here are very different from those who come from the So: & Wes:
these are call'd here Savages[.]

Bibliography

Abler, Thomas S., and Elisabeth Tooker. "Seneca." In *Handbook of North American Indians*. Vol. 15, *Northeast*, edited by Bruce G. Trigger, 505–17. Washington, DC: Smithsonian Institution, 1978.

Adreani, Paolo. "Travels of a Gentleman from Milan." In *In Mohawk Country: Narratives of a Native People*, edited by Dean R. Snow, Charles T. Gehring, and William A. Starna, 318–33. Syracuse: Syracuse University Press, 1996.

Bain, James, ed., *Travels and Adventures in Canada and the Indian Territories Between the Years 1760 and 1776, by Alexander Henry, Fur Trader*. Boston: Little, Brown, 1901.

Barker, William V. H. *Early Families of Herkimer County, New York*. Baltimore: Genealogical Publishing, 1986.

Bartlett, John Russell. *History of the Wanton Family of Newport, Rhode Island*. Providence: Sidney and Rider, 1878.

Beauvoir, François-Jean de, Marquis de Chastellux. "Visit to Schenectady, 1780." In *In Mohawk Country: Narratives of a Native People*, edited by Dean R. Snow, Charles T. Gehring, and William A. Starna, 292–94. Syracuse: Syracuse University Press, 1996.

Belknap, Jeremy. *The History of New Hampshire. . . .*, vol. 2. Dover: O. Crosby and J. Varney, 1812.

Benson, Adolph B., rev. and ed. *Peter Kalm's Travels in North America: The English Version of 1770*. New York: Dover, 1987.

Blau, Harold, Jack Campisi, and Elisabeth Tooker. "Onondaga." In *Handbook of North American Indians*. Vol. 15, *Northeast*, edited by Bruce G. Trigger, 491–99. Washington, DC: Smithsonian Institution, 1978.

Bloomfield, Joseph. "Journal of Joseph Bloomfield." In *In Mohawk Country: Narratives of a Native People*, edited by Dean R. Snow, Charles T. Gehring, and William A. Starna, 274–91. Syracuse: Syracuse University Press, 1996.

Calloway, Colin G. *The American Revolution in Indian Country: Crisis and Diversity in Native American Communities*. Cambridge: Cambridge University Press, 1995.

———. "Fort Niagara: The Politics of Hunger in a Refugee Community." In *The American Revolution in Indian Country: Crisis and Diversity in Native American Communities*. Cambridge: Cambridge University Press, 1995, 129–57.

Campisi, Jack. "Oneida." In *Handbook of North American Indians*. Vol. 15, *Northeast*, edited by Bruce G. Trigger, 481–90. Washington, DC: Smithsonian Institution, 1978.

———. "From Stanwix to Canandaigua: National Policy, States' Rights, and Indian Land." In *Iroquois Land Claims*, edited by Christopher Vecsey and William A. Starna, 49–65. Syracuse: Syracuse University Press, 1988.

Carretta, Vincent. *Phyllis Wheatley: Biography of a Genius in Bondage*. Athens: University of Georgia Press, 2011.

Cook, Frederick. *Journals of the Military Expedition of Major John Sullivan Against the Six Nations of Indians in 1779 with Records of Centennial Celebrations*. Auburn: Knapp, Peck, and Thomson, 1887.

Dictionary of Canadian Biography, 15 vols. Toronto: University of Toronto Press, 1967–2005. http://www.biographi.ca/en/index.php.

Dix, John Ross. *A Hand-book of Newport, and Rhode Island*. Newport: C. E. Hammett, Jr., 1852.

Doblin, Helga, and William A. Starna, eds. and trans. *The Journals of Christian Daniel Claus and Conrad Weiser: A Journal to Onondaga, 1750*. Philadelphia: American Philosophical Society, 1994.

Fenton, William N. "The Journal of James Emlen Kept on a Trip to Canandaigua, New York." *Ethnohistory* 12, no. 4 (1965): 279–342.

———. *The Great Law and the Longhouse: A Political History of the Iroquois Confederacy*. Norman: University of Oklahoma Press, 1998.

Fenton, William N., and Elisabeth Tooker. "Mohawk." In *Handbook of North American Indians*. Vol. 15, *Northeast*, edited by Bruce G. Trigger, 466–80. Washington, DC: Smithsonian Institution, 1978.

[Fisher, Jabez Maud], "More Galloway Letters." *Historical Magazine* July 1862: 204–05.

Fleming, R. H. "Phyn, Ellice and Company of Schenectady." *Contributions to Canadian Economics* 4 (1932): 7–41.

Frey, Samuel Ludlow, ed. *The Minute Book of the Committee of Safety of Tryon County....* New York: Dodd, Mead, 1905.

Gordon, Thomas F. *A Gazetteer of the State of New Jersey ... Accompanied by a Map*. Trenton, NJ: Daniel Fenton, 1834.

Graymont, Barbara. *The Iroquois in the American Revolution*. Syracuse: Syracuse University Press, 1972.

Halsey, Francis W., ed. *A Tour of the Hudson, the Mohawk, the Susquehanna, and the Delaware in 1769, Being the Journal of Richard Smith of Burlington, New Jersey*. 1906. Reprint, Fleischmanns NY: Purple Mountain Press, 1989.

Hough, Franklin B., ed. and trans. *Memoir Upon the Late War Between the French and English, 1755–1760 ... by M. Pouchot*, vol. 2. Roxbury: W. Elliot Woodward, 1866.

Johnson, Warren. "Journal of Warren Johnson." In *In Mohawk Country: Narratives of a Native People*, edited by Dean R. Snow, Charles T. Gehring, and William A. Starna, 250–73. Syracuse: Syracuse University Press, 1996.

Johnson, William, Sir. *Papers of Sir William Johnson*, 14 vols. Edited by James Sullivan et al. Albany: University of the State of New York, 1921–62.

Knowles, Nathaniel. "The Torture of Captives by the Indians of Eastern North America." *Proceedings of the American Philosophical Society* 82, no. 2 (1940): 151–225.

Kurath, Gertrude Prokosch. *Iroquois Music and Dance: Ceremonial Arts of Two Seneca Longhouses*. Bureau of American Ethnology Bulletin 187. Washington, DC: U. S. Government Printing Office, 1964.

Landy, David. "Tuscarora Among the Iroquois." In *Handbook of North American Indians*. Vol. 15, *Northeast*, edited by Bruce G. Trigger, 518–24. Washington, DC: Smithsonian Institution, 1978.

Lord, Philip, Jr. "Taverns, Forts, and Castles: Rediscovering Hendrick's Village." *Northeast Anthropology* 52 (1996): 69–94.

Lounsbury, Floyd G., "Iroquois Place-Names in the Champlain Valley." In *Neighbors and Intruders: An Ethnohistorical Exploration of the Indians of Hudson's River*, edited by Laurence M. Hauptman and Jack Campisi, 103–49. Canadian Ethnological Services, Paper 39. Ottawa: National Museum of Man, 1978.

Lydekker, John Wolfe. *The Faithful Mohawks*. Port Washington: Ira J. Friedman, 1938.

Mackey, Frank. *Black Then: Blacks and Montreal, 1780s–1880s*. Kingston: McGill-Queen's University Press, 2004.

Marbois, François. "Journey to the Oneidas, 1784." In *In Mohawk Country: Narratives of a Native People*, edited by Dean R. Snow, Charles T. Gehring, and William A. Starna, 300–17. Syracuse: Syracuse University Press, 1996.

Marino, Cesare, and Karim M. Tiro, eds. and trans. *Along the Hudson and Mohawk: The 1790 Journey of Count Paolo Andreani*. Philadelphia: University of Pennsylvania Press, 2006.

Mathews, William, comp., with Roy Harvey Pearce. *American Diaries: An Annotated Bibliography of American Diaries Written Before 1861*. Berkeley: University of California Press, 1945.

Morgan, Kenneth, ed. *An American Quaker in the British Isles: The Travel Journals of Jabez Maud Fisher, 1775–1779*. New York: Oxford University Press, 1992.

Nelson, Paul David. *William Tryon and the Course of Empire: A Life in the British Imperial Service*. Chapel Hill: University of North Carolina Press, 1994.

O'Toole, Fintan. *White Savage: William Johnson and the Invention of America.* Albany: State University of New York Press, 2009.

Peterson, Edward. *History of Rhode Island and Newport.* New York: John S. Taylor, 1853.

Riley, Carroll L. "The Blowgun in the New World." *Southwestern Journal of Anthropology* 8, no. 3 (1952): 297–319.

Sabine, Lorenzo. *Biographical Sketches of Loyalists of the American Revolution, with an Historical Essay by Lorenzo Sabine,* 2 vols. Boston: Little, Brown, 1864.

Sailly, Peter. "Diary of Peter Sailly on a Journey in American in the Year 1784." In *In Mohawk Country: Narratives of a Native People,* edited by Dean R. Snow, Charles T. Gehring, and William A. Starna, 295–99. Syracuse: Syracuse University Press, 1996.

Savery, William. *A Journal of the Life, Travels, and Religious Labours of William Savery.* Comp. Jonathan Evans. C. Gilpin: London, 1844.

Scott, John Albert. *Fort Stanwix (Fort Schuyler) and Oriskany . . . .* Rome: Rome Sentinel Company, 1927.

Shannon, Timothy. "Dressing for Success on the Mohawk Frontier: Hendrick, William Johnson, and the Indian Fashion." *William and Mary Quarterly* 53, no. 1(1996): 13–42.

Silver, Peter. *Our Savage Neighbors: How Indian War Transformed Early America.* New York: W. W. Norton, 2008.

Smith, Anna Wharton. *Genealogy of the Fisher Family, 1682 to 1896.* Philadelphia, 1896.

Snow, Dean R. *Mohawk Valley Archaeology: The Sites.* The Institute for Archaeological Studies. Albany: University at Albany, State University of New York, 1995.

Stanwood, James Rindge. *The Direct Ancestry of the Late Jacob Wendell . . . .* Boston: David Clapp and Son, 1882.

Starna, William A., and Jack Campisi. "When Two Are One: The Mohawk Indian Community at St. Regis (Akwesasne)." *European Review of Native American Studies* 14, no. 2 (2000): 39–45.

Stewart, W. Brian. *The Ermatingers: A Nineteenth-Century Ojibwa-Canadian Family.* Vancouver: University of British Columbia Press, 2007.

Syrett, Harold C., ed. *The Papers of Alexander Hamilton,* vol. 19. New York: Columbia University Press, 1973.

Syrett, Harold C., and Jacob E. Cooke, eds. *The Papers of Alexander Hamilton,* vol. 15. New York: Columbia University Press, 1969.

Taylor, Alan. *The Divided Ground: Indians, Settlers, and the Northern Borderland of the American Revolution.* New York: Alfred A. Knopf, 2006.

Thompson, James. *The Seasons.* London: T. Longman, B. Law and Son, etc., 1793.

Tiro, Karim M. *The People of the Standing Stone: The Oneida Nation from the Revolution Through the Era of Removal*. Amherst: The University of Massachusetts Press, 2011.

White, Marian E., William E. Engelbrecht, and Elisabeth Tooker. "Cayuga." In *Handbook of North American Indians*. Vol. 15, *Northeast*, edited by Bruce G. Trigger, 500–04. Washington, DC: Smithsonian Institution, 1978.

Wood, Sumner Gilbert. *The Taverns and Turnpikes of Blandford, 1733–1833*. Published by the author, 1908.

Index

www.ingramcontent.com/pod-product-compliance
Lightning Source LLC
Chambersburg PA
CBHW080928100426
42812CB00007B/2408